BLACK+DECKER™

HOME
PLANNER&
LOGBOOK

Quarto is the authority on a wide range of topics.

Quarto educates, entertains and enriches the lives of our readers—enthusiasts and lovers of hands-on living.

www.quartoknows.com

© 2015 Quarto Publishing Group USA Inc.

First published in 2015 by Cool Springs Press, an imprint of Quarto Publishing Group USA Inc., 400 First Avenue North, Suite 400, Minneapolis, MN 55401 USA. Telephone: (612) 344-8100 Fax: (612) 344-8692

quartoknows.com
Visit our blogs at quartoknows.com

Cool Springs Press titles are also available at discounts in bulk quantity for industrial or sales-promotional use. For details contact the Special Sales Manager at Quarto Publishing Group USA Inc., 400 First Avenue North, Suite 400, Minneapolis, MN 55401 USA.

10 9 8 7 6 5 4 3 2 1

ISBN: 978-1-59186-646-6

Acquiring Editor: Mark Johanson
Project Manager: Alyssa Bluhm
Art Directors: Brad Springer and Alexandra Burniece
Cover Designer: Simon Larkin
Layout: Diana Boger
Author: Chris Peterson
Images courtesy of Shutterstock: Cover, 7, 9, 10, 11, 13, 15 (right, all), 17 (all), 22, 23 (top), 24 (top, middle), 27 (right), 31 (top), 32, 39 (both), 43, 47

Printed in China

NOTICE TO READERS

For safety, use caution, care, and good judgment when following the procedures described in this book. The publisher and BLACK+DECKER cannot assume responsibility for any damage to property or injury to persons as a result of misuse of the information provided.

The techniques shown in this book are general techniques for various applications. In some instances, additional techniques not shown in this book may be required. Always follow manufacturers' instructions included with products, since deviating from the directions may void warranties. The projects in this book vary widely as to skill levels required: some may not be appropriate for all do-it-yourselfers, and some may require professional help.

Consult your local building department for information on building permits, codes, and other laws as they apply to your project.

HOME PLANNER& LOGBOOK

Record all your important information for easy, one-stop reference

Chris Peterson

COOL SPRINGS PRESS

Home and Garden Experts™

MINNEAPOLIS, MINNESOTA

Contents

Introduction

If you're an established homeowner, you already know this; if you're a new homeowner, you're about to learn it: a home is a complex creature with many systems and components, and within a few years you will find it necessary to fix many elements, repair some, and replace others. A home is a living structure in constant transition and evolution, static for no more than a few weeks or months at a time, even in the best of times.

Some people never organize a detailed history of repairs or replacements, and for others, their home repair and replacement records are stored in loose files tucked away in a desk drawer somewhere. It is far easier, though, if you can document in one single spot all the specifications, record all the dates, note the various warranties, and log in the names and contact information for the various repairmen and contractors you will come to rely on. Even if you are an avid do-it-yourselfer, it's far better to have one place to record things like paint colors of your living room walls, the make and model number of your faucets and clothes washer, the contact information for city inspection offices and the sewer service guy you used last time the floor drains plugged up.

That's where the *BLACK+DECKER Home Planner & Logbook* comes to the rescue. Not only is the book an all-in-one repository for keeping track of all the important repair and replacement details on your home, but it also is a guided tour for discovering that information. Along the way, you'll learn more about your home than you ever thought possible, becoming *the* expert.

This book is organized in four segments. In the first three, Understanding Your Home, Your Home's Systems, and Your Appliances, you'll get a whirlwind tour of the various components and systems of a home that need ongoing vigilance, inspection, and maintenance. These are organized with intuitive logic, starting from the roof, moving down to the foundations and landscape; then moving indoors to examine the structural and surface elements, like the walls and floors, and finally examining the appliances and other add-ons.

In the fourth section, Home Logbook, you'll find the journal itself, where you can conveniently document everything you need to record about what has been done to your home or who to call when your home needs attention. And you'll also learn what to watch for and how often you should inspect the various elements. Organized in the same order as the opening sections, the logbook is incredibly easy to navigate, and when emergencies or unexpected events occur, you'll be able to pull down this book from your shelf and instantly know who to call for help.

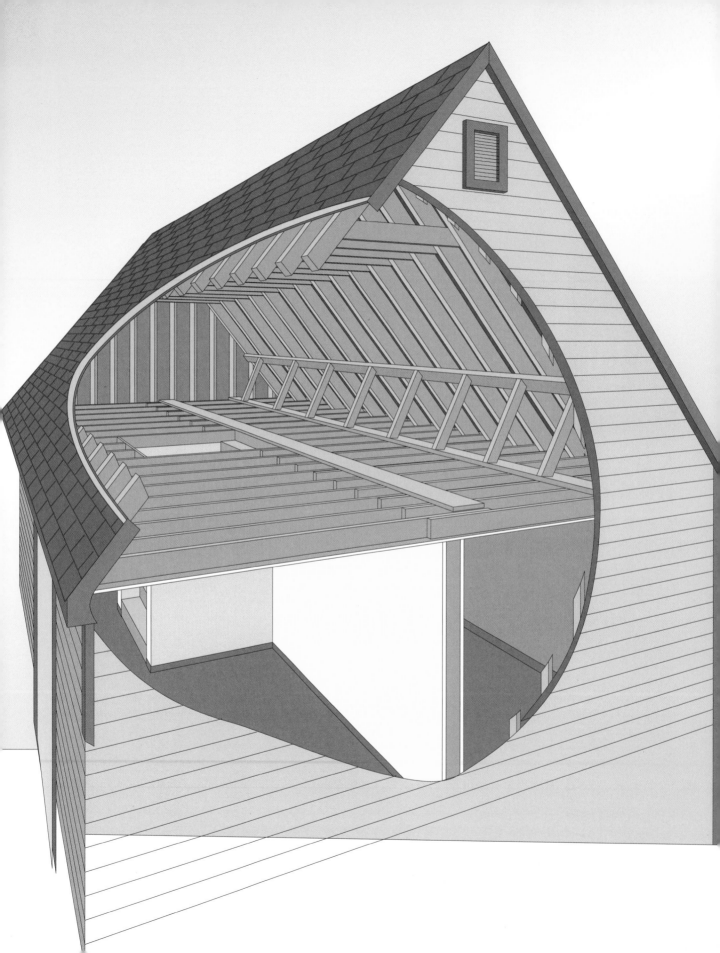

Section 1 | Understanding Your Home

Your home—any home—is a combination of a structure and systems that work in tandem to make a comfortable, usable living space. Getting to know your home means visually inspecting the structure and checking the individual systems that run throughout that structure.

Any comprehensive inspection begins at the top and works down, the same way elemental forces act on the building. Follow the first three sections from start to finish and they will take you through a complete overview of the elements covered in the fourth section, the Home Logbook. You'll start with the structure and then move on to inspecting your systems and appliances. This will mean retracing your steps in some instances, but it's the best way to form an overall picture of your home's current health and potential trouble spots. Particular things to keep an eye out for include:

- **Structural interactions.** Notice how different parts of the building work together in unison. For instance, the walls hold up the roof, and the roof protects the wall framing from water. Windows and doors can help or hurt the insulating value of the walls.
- **Obvious damage.** Aside from what you'll make note of, you may come across larger problems—a hole in the roof from squirrels, for instance. These should be remedied immediately.

Dress right for the inspection. You want to be comfortable, but you also want to be protected from the occasional sharp edge, loose screw, and other dangers. You'll be getting dirty; something to keep in mind when choosing appropriate garb. Carry safety glasses and a dust mask. Wear a hat (a hard hat would not be overkill). Suit up with long sleeves and long pants rugged enough to hold up to abuse. Wear work boots or, at the very least, rugged shoes that completely cover the foot and provide some ankle support. You'll also want to don heavy-duty work gloves.

INSPECTION TOOLS & EQUIPMENT

Binoculars (optional)

Structural Inspection:
Awl
Pencil
This book
Measuring tape
Level
Ladder

Systems Inspection:
Outlet tester
Screwdrivers (Phillips and standard)

COLLECTING CRITICAL DOCUMENTS

Use the pockets at the back of this book for physical copies of important paperwork, but keep critical documents that would be difficult to replace in a centrally located, locked, fireproof container. Run down the list of documents below to make sure you have physical copies. If you don't already own a fireproof lock box or safe, buy one—or keep the documents in a safety deposit box at your bank. If ever it protects your documents from fire or flood, it will seem like the world's smartest investment.

- ❏ Copy of title
- ❏ Copy of deed
- ❏ Homeowner's insurance policy (including your agent contact information)
- ❏ Copies of liens
- ❏ Proof of loan payoff
- ❏ Home Inventory (see page 112)
- ❏ Safe deposit box inventory and key
- ❏ Records of zone variances
- ❏ Birth certificates (yours and your children's)
- ❏ Life insurance policies
- ❏ Will
- ❏ Diplomas

Your Roof

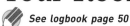

See logbook page 50

Your home inspection starts with the roof because it's the home's primary defense against the elements, especially water. Any problem with the roof structure can lead to problems in all the other systems and structures. Inspect it regularly, note changes, and call a professional immediately whenever you detect serious problems.

Begin by visually checking all areas of the roof. You can do much of this inspection with a pair of good binoculars, but there really is no substitute for getting on the roof and looking closely at shingles and trouble spots such as chimney flashing. Be aware that some types of roofing should not be walked on, such as membrane and tile roofs. If you have any doubts, contact the original manufacturer (or look them up online) or consult a local roofer.

It's especially helpful if you can figure out when the roof was installed and determine if there is an existing warranty. Residential roofs last 15 to 30 years, depending on the material used, the level of craftsmanship, and the local climate. Warranties typically run 15 to 20 years. Twenty years is a good outer limit for roof life, at which point you should look very carefully for problems and begin considering replacement.

Even if you can't determine the age, a careful close examination will give you a good idea of the condition. Inspect your roof yearly and after any significant storm or weather event. The inspection should go hand-in-hand with inspecting the gutters and drainage system (see page 12).

IDENTIFY YOUR ROOF TYPE

There are five basic types of residential roofs.

1. **Asphalt shingle.** The least expensive and most popular roofing. The shingles are comprised of substrate impregnated with asphalt. Signs of deterioration include buckling, splitting, and shedding of asphalt granules (finding granules in gutters is often the first sign of asphalt shingle failure).

2. **Wooden shingle/shake.** These roofs vary widely in quality and longevity. **Look for:** splitting, curling, and growth of lichen, moss, mold, mildew, or algae—all of which are common signs of wood roof deterioration.

3. **Tile.** Most roof tiles are made from terra-cotta or hardened clay. Uniform tile spacing and color are signs of a roof in good condition. **Look for:** loose or broken tiles, which allow water infiltration. Check for color variations that signal the tiles are breaking down and absorbing water, including white "efflorescence," green moss and algae, and dark mold stains. All these signs indicate tiles that are close to failure.

4. **Slate.** Slate tiles are mechanically fastened to the underlying structure. That means failure is obvious in tiles that are cracked, missing, or out of pattern with the rest of the roof. Repairs must be made immediately to avoid damage that compromises the underlying structure. Properly maintained slate roofs can last up to 100 years.

5. **Metal.** Rust spots or rust lines are obvious signs of concern. Corrosion, misshapen sections, missing fasteners or roof sections all indicate serious problems. Discoloration is a sign that the metal roof is at the end of its life.

3

4

BE SAFE!
Walking on a roof is not recommended. But if you do, always wear shoes with nonskid soles and tie off to some sort of fall-arrest harness. Home centers stock low-cost, quality harnesses and leashes, so there's just no excuse to skip this valuable precaution.

5

Your Gutters, Downspouts, Soffits & Vents

 *See logbook page 51*

Gutters and downspouts form a system for directing water away from the home, and especially away from the foundation. It is a simple system, but incredibly essential. One small leak can, over time, lead to damages that could cost thousands of dollars to repair. It's always easier and cheaper to keep an eye on your gutters and downspouts and jump on repairs as soon as you detect a problem.

Professionals recommend inspecting your gutters twice a year, although you should also check them right after any major weather event (especially if that event included freezing temperatures).

An inspection usually involves cleaning the gutters so that you can visually check every surface and part. Clogged gutters are a major source of water problems, so cleaning them regularly goes hand-in-hand with inspection in preventing problems before.

Soffits are the underside of the eaves, while fascia are the boards that form the front of the eaves between the roof joist ends. Some houses feature open soffits without fascia. But in many homes, the soffits are enclosed. Check soffits and fascia for rot. If they are metal, check for rust or other damage. Also check gable or soffit vents. These are how your roof breathes so that air circulates and moisture doesn't accumulate. Once you have cleaned the gutters, follow these inspection steps, and note the results of your inspection:

1. **Bracket or hanger integrity. Look for:** brackets that are missing; bent; rusted; pulling away; sagging.
2. **Gutter condition and slope.** Check gutter slope with a level. Ideally, each run should slope to a downspout 1/8 inch per foot. Also inspect inside the gutters. **Look for:** mid-run sagging; holes; rot; corrosion; separating seams; other damage or deformity.
3. **Gutter covers/screens.** If your gutters have covers or leaf screens, **look for:** missing sections; blockages; rust, rot or corrosion; sagging/deformity.
4. **Downspouts.** Any downspout should be securely fastened to the gutter outlet and should run down to an elbow over a concrete or plastic splash tray or extension that leads water away from the house. **Look for:** compromised seams; rust, rot, or deterioration; missing extension or bottom elbow; missing splash tray.
5. **Soffits and fascia.** Soffit covers and fascia should be secure and free of damage or stains. **Look for:** missing soffit boards or screens and missing fascia; water stains; wet or dry rot (probe with an awl); physical damage such as bent metal soffit covers.
6. **Soffit and gable vents.** The vent cover screens should be unobstructed. **Look for:** blocked vent screen or opening; damaged screen or opening; missing screens or sign of animal activity.

BE SAFE!
Inspecting roofs and gutters inevitably means climbing a ladder. Follow these rules to make sure your home inspection doesn't become an emergency-room adventure:

- Make sure a stepladder is set level and opened fully with the locking hinge secured.
- Never step on the top two steps of a stepladder.
- Set an extension ladder one rung's distance out from the wall for every four rungs of height.
- Secure an extension ladder with nonslip feet or a brace, and make sure the top is leaning against a stable, secure surface.
- Project the extension ladder at least three rungs above where it contacts the roof or gutter.
- Tie off any securing rope the ladder is equipped with.
- Engage all locks on the ladder prior to using.

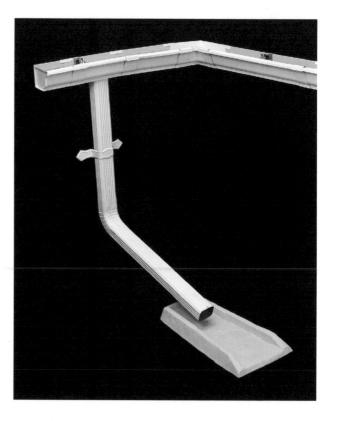

Your Siding

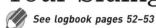

See logbook pages 52–53

Siding is a home's protective skin and the key barrier against the elements penetrating walls and undermining the framing. Unfortunately, siding is so obvious that most homeowners only notice a glaring problem. But the best time to remedy a siding issue is before it looms large.

That means checking the siding regularly. Do this in spring, when any damage from winter weather will be most apparent. All siding should also be cleaned once a year. It's easiest to do this when you inspect it. What you'll be looking for depends on the siding material.

1. **Stucco.** Applied and maintained correctly, stucco siding can last more than 50 years. However stucco is porous, so it can actually conceal moisture-related issues. The surface is also irregular and, under the right conditions, can serve as a base for mold, mildew, or algae. Ensure the longevity of stucco siding by painting it with an *elastomeric* paint formulated for use on masonry—especially when painting over repairs. **Look for:** hairline cracks around joints and seams such at door or window frames; missing sections that have fallen off the wall; staining or discoloration; mold or mildew.

2. **Stone and brick.** The weak link in any stone or brick siding is the mortar. Mortar lines are prone to cracking and crumbling over time, leaving the wall surface susceptible to moisture. Inspect for even small cracks. Brick varies in quality but all brick has a limited life span. Deteriorating brick may require wholesale replacement. Because they are absorbent to one degree or another, brick and stones are also prone to mold and algae growth on wet, north-facing surfaces. **Look for:** mortar cracks; missing mortar; missing bricks or stones; crumbling or flaking bricks (known as "spalling"); mold, algae, or mildew.

3. **Aluminum.** Before vinyl, aluminum was considered the "miracle siding." It doesn't rust, so experts believed this siding would last forever. The truth is, properly maintained, aluminum could theoretically last the life the house. Chalking paint is natural and can often be alleviated with a good washing. If not, it may be time to paint—always use a zinc oxide primer and a top coat that is meant for metal. Paint aluminum siding with a spray gun. **Look for:** chalking; missing corners, end sections, or panels; compromised fasteners, apparent in misalignment of individual siding panels; dents.

4. **Vinyl.** Vinyl is an incredibly durable plastic, easy to mold and long lasting. Unfortunately is does fade and, depending on the type, fasteners may fail over time. As with aluminum, vinyl siding should be washed at least once a year. Generally, it is never repainted. If you want to change the color or freshen the look, you should hire a professional. **Look for:** loose or missing corners, caps, or panels; sagging panels caused by fastener failure; cracks or tears; drips or marks that could reveal a problem behind the siding.

5. **Wood.** Wood is considered some of the most beautiful and high-maintenance siding. Different types include flat panels, overlapping shingles, and clapboard. Different woods offer varying levels of protection against rot, cracking, and insect damage. Wood siding should be painted at least every five years, or whenever the paint looks worn. Wood is prone to more problems than other siding because it contracts and expands, and it is naturally absorbent. **Look for:** peeling paint or finish; cracking, splitting or warping; missing shingles, corners, or trim; rot or water damage; insect holes or other signs of infestation.

6. **Cement fiber.** Cement fiber lap siding may not be readily recognizable, because it looks so much like wood lap siding or textured vinyl siding. It is now available in lap siding, shingles, vertical pieces for a board-and-batten look, even trim and soffit components. It is a very heavy and durable material, but its Achilles' heel is the unfinished edges, which, over time, can absorb moisture and swell. Upkeep on cement fiber siding is really about keeping the seams and edges caulked to prevent this, and occasionally painting when the current paint job fades. Painting chores will be considerably infrequent, though, because cement fiber holds paint very well, without the bubbling or peeling that sometimes happens with wood.

Your Door & Window Framing

 See logbook pages 54–57

Windows and doors are naturally weak links in wall surfaces, lowering the insulation value and providing yet another avenue for water and insects. Of course, that's a necessary tradeoff—doors allow movement into and out of the home, and windows provide essential light and air.

Start by checking around the frame of each door and window. Gaps need to be addressed immediately. Use your awl to probe wood sills, door thresholds, and the bottoms and edges of doors. Note cracks or failed window seals. Older, single-pane windows need to be regularly re-puttied (removing and replacing old putty can drastically increase insulation value), so look for cracking, curling, and missing putty.

- **Caulking.** Caulking creates an essential seal. Even the best caulk deteriorates over time and will need replacement. Caulk should completely cover a joint or seam, and should be secured to the underlying surface. **Look for:** missing or cracked caulk; caulking no longer adhering to underlying surface; discoloration.
- **Hardware.** Handles, locks, hinges, and other hardware must be sound. Door hardware, especially, is a matter of safety. **Look for:** loose or missing screws or fasteners; hinges with too much play; loose door handles; locks with too much play (could be forced); rusting or corrosion.

- **Seals and putty.** The seal between glass and window structure in an insulated window is often the first part to fail. Putty dries out over time, cracking and eventually failing. Seals in lower-cost double-insulated windows tend to fail with age, allowing air and moisture into the space between panes. Door and window weather stripping compresses and wears under day-to-day use. **Look for:** fogging or condensation inside an insulated window; crumbling, cracking, curling, or missing window putty on a single-paned window; cracked, torn, compressed, or missing weather stripping; obvious gaps around a closed door.
- **Door and window structures. Look for:** cracks; door or window askew in the opening; holes (i.e., missing peepholes, empty drill holes, etc.); rot; deteriorating paint.
- **Frame, trim, sills, and thresholds.** The pieces that surround a door and window are most often wood. Given the exposure and heavy use, these elements are prone to deterioration. **Look for:** large cracks; separation from underlying framing; excessive wear; worn paint; holes from screws or nails; insect damage or infiltration; dry or wet rot.

Your Windows

See logbook pages 54–55

The integrity of your home's windows can have a radical effect on energy costs. Windows that maintain a tight seal and conduct little heat or cold help reduce heating and cooling expenses. Windows in poor condition do the opposite. Except for fixed windows, most windows are partnered with an insect screen or storm window—or an aluminum combination unit that combines both. If the insect screens and storm windows are individual separate units, they are typically changed out each season, a convenient time to inspect them and make any necessary repairs. In more modern insulated window units, no secondary storm window is needed, and the insect screens may well be integrated into the window unit itself.

Window frames—both the structure holding the glass and larger, overall structure in which the window is installed—can be wood, metal, fiberglass, vinyl, or a combination. Wood is prone to insect infestation, rot, water damage, and cracking. Metal frames can bend out of shape, rust, or corrode. Vinyl frames may be deformed by exposure to heat and will also become brittle and less pliable over time. Fiberglass is expensive but durable.

Check both the window and the framing around the opening. Check that windows open and close correctly, and feel for airflow when the window is closed.

1. **Casement.** This type opens out from one side, using a screw-type handle. The handle's action should be smooth and silent. Two variations are used in special situations and locations: the hopper opens top out, and the transom or awning, opens bottom out. **Look for:** window closing off-kilter in frame; warped window rail or stile; stuck or stripped crank; sagging hinge; incomplete seal around the closed window; window sticks; cracked glass; fogged glass.

2. **Bypass.** Also known as "sliding windows," these slide open and shut in a channel. **Look for:** window sticking in the channel; deformed or corroding channel; gaps between glass and rails or stiles; window cocked in channel; gaps when window is closed; cracked glass, fogged glass.

3. **Double hanging and single hanging.** The window is divided into two halves, the bottom opening upward in front of the top half. Counterbalance weights in older double hanging windows often break loose and fall into the frame enclosure. **Look for:** broken weight cords; windows painted shut; warped frame channels causing sticking and jamming; dry or wet rot; cracking or separating of the panes from the rails and stiles; lock misaligned; cracked glass; fogged glass.

4. **Fixed.** Fixed windows come in many shapes and sizes. **Look for:** separation between glass and surrounding frame; compromised seals; cracked glass; fogged glass.

5. **Specialized windows.** Such as jalousie or other louvered or center-pivot windows. **Look for:** jammed or sticking opening mechanism; misalignment that causes the window to close improperly; cracked glass; fogged glass.

6. **Screens.** Window screens have wood, metal, or vinyl frames, and metal or fiberglass screening. The two main problems common to all screens are twisting or warping and holes. **Look for:** small or large punctures or tears; frames that won't lay flat; fraying where screening attaches to the frame.

Your Walkways, Driveway & Steps

 *See logbook page 59*

Concrete paths, driveways, sidewalks, and entry steps may not be as permanent as you think. All concrete structures will degrade with time, and cracks, separations, or heaving can be an indication of soil instability or foundational problems with adjoining structures. Proper concrete installations will be laid on a bed of gravel (below) to prevent seasonal heaving, but improper installation may cause problems after only a few years.

Large cracks are a cause for concern. Driveways are sloped away from the home because they must direct water away from the foundation. A large crack allows water to potentially undermine the foundation. A quick inspection will help you determine the state of any paved pathways, sidewalks, and the driveway. Cement caulk and vinyl patching cement products (below) are easy to use, and an annual inspection cycle and repairs when needed can forestall the need for replacement many years.

- **Sidewalks.** In most municipalities, the homeowner is responsible for sidewalks in front of the home. Sidewalks that are not level are a tripping hazard that could lead to homeowner liability. **Look for:** uneven sidewalk surface; persistent moss, algae, or slickness.

- **Driveways and other asphalt or concrete surfaces.** Driveways and thin concrete slabs under sheds or garbage cans are prone to cracking. Small cracks are not a problem. Any crack that goes all the way through the surface should be repaired. Asphalt driveways should also be resealed every two to three years, and cracks should be filled with crack filler as they appear. **Look for:** large, deep cracks going down to soil; deep indentions that might indicate soil erosion due to an underlying drainage problem; heaving.

- **Entry steps.** Steps made from concrete are subject to some of the same problems as other concrete surfaces. Settling or pulling away from foundations can be a sign of more serious structural problems, and over time they may simply degrade due to years of seasonal stress. If you are in a home long enough, you can expect to replace concrete steps at some point, though regular inspection and repair can greatly lengthen their life span.

Your Deck, Patio & Porch

See logbook pages 60–61

Decks, patios, and porches are very often attached to the house along at least one side via a ledger board (photo, right). Points of attachment represent potential weak spots. These structures should also be sloped away from the house to direct water away from the foundation. Time and wear and errors in construction can produce the opposite—a connected structure that slopes back toward the house. That means the first thing to inspect is slope. Hold a four-foot level along the surface of the patio, deck, or porch, and check out to the edge. The ideal slope should be about 1/4 inch per foot.

- **Porch.** The most complicated of these structures, a porch includes a roof connected to the house and a frame often tied to a foundation wall. Because it is covered, the deck slope is not as essential as it is with a deck or patio. However, insect infestations often start with rotted wood in the porch. House-side attachments can be entry points for water. **Look for:** failing connections along the ledger that connects the porch deck to the house; missing or compromised lag screws or bolts; ledger separation from the house wall, or gaps between ledger and wall; compromised post-and-pier supports; rodent tunnels or gnaw marks; signs of insect infestations, such as termite tubes; failing structural members such as steps or rails. If the porch roof is equipped with gutters, inspect them as well. Follow the guidelines on page 12.
- **Deck.** Decks are usually positioned right outside a back door. Although many deck builders butt the deck up to the house but build it freestanding, most existing decks are attached along a ledger—essentially a rim joist attached to the house and serving as the anchor for the side of the deck butting against the house. Many ledgers are improperly attached, and even correctly installed ledgers are prone to failed fasteners. When a ledger pulls away from the house, it can cause deck collapse and extensive damage to the house. Ledgers should be connected with lag screws or bolts and nuts (if there's access to the other side of the wall) with washers. Pay close attention to the flashing between the top of the ledger and the house. This is a potential pathway for water. Get underneath to inspect the deck. **Look for:** ledger firmly attached to the house; ledger fasteners compromised or missing; joist hangers compromised, or lacking nails; corroded fasteners; loose or broken deck boards; dry or wet rot (probe with an awl); wood

absorbing water; insect infestation or damage; broken or bowing support post or beam; crumbling or sinking foundation pier.
- **Patio.** The most important thing for any patio is for it to slope away from the house. Other problems will likely affect only the patio itself. **Look for:** concrete spalling, crumbling, or cracking; paver heaving or sinking; missing sand around pavers (replace with polymer sand for more stability).

Your Landscape Features

See logbook pages 62–63

Exterior structures such as fences or garden walls can have an unusually large impact on property value. That impact can be negative when the structure is in poor condition. These barriers can also be important for keeping wildlife out of a yard and garden. The primary inspection tool is a carpenter's level.

Of nearly equal importance are the other hardscape features of your landscape, such as retaining walls, and outbuildings such as sheds, garages, and gazebos. Finally, there is the "living landscape"—trees, hedges, garden plantings, and the lawn itself. All of these are integral to a working home and are worthy of the same diligence as the structure and systems of the home itself.

- **Fences.** Fences range from purely ornamental to purely functional. They can be built of many different materials, but all fences share common features. These include support posts secured in the ground, horizontal rails that tie posts together and from which are hung the fencing (balusters, pickets, or boards). **Look for:** posts out of plumb; rotted or cracked in-ground post support; insect damage; post-end decomposition; loose, missing, or damaged fencing; warped pickets or balusters; missing decorative finials; loose or damaged rails; large sections of rust; worn, peeling, or missing paint; entire fence out of plumb.

- **Gates.** Gates are more prone to wear and failure than other fence or wall parts. **Look for:** loose hinge(s); squeaking hinge; loose or missing hinge fasteners; loose or missing latch or catch; misaligned latch and catch; damaged rail(s); loose, missing, or damaged pickets or balusters.

- **Walls.** Garden and yard walls are usually built up from a trench footing rather than support posts. They are also solid—most commonly brick or stone. **Look for:** missing stone or bricks; concrete or brick spalling; compromised mortar joints; sections severely out of plumb or about to fall; sinking wall foundation (dips in the top surface); complete wall failure.

- **Garages, sheds, gazebos.** These structural features have many of the same issues as the home itself, and you should routinely inspect and document the condition and repairs for roofs, walls, windows, and doors. A garage will of course have the same issues, but also will have a large garage door operated by a mechanical motor. Having your garage door technician's vital information at ready access is always a good idea.

- **Hardscaping.** This catchall term includes the various permanent features of a landscape, such retaining walls, ponds and swimming pools, garden edgings, raised beds, and other constructed features. Once a year, at minimum, you'll need to inspect these, as well, and keep notes on their condition and service history.

- **Softscaping.** This term includes the "living" landscape—the trees, shrubs and hedges, the planting areas and flower beds, and even the lawn itself. As any experienced homeowner will tell you, tending to things like pruning, watering, weeding, and fertilizing can make a huge difference in the livability quotient of your home—not to mention its resale value. You should document the maintenance and upkeep of your living landscape in much the same way as the structural elements. **Look for:** lawns or garden beds filled with weeds or showing signs of diseases; shrubs that are overgrown or barren; trees with dead or broken branches, or badly in need of trimming.

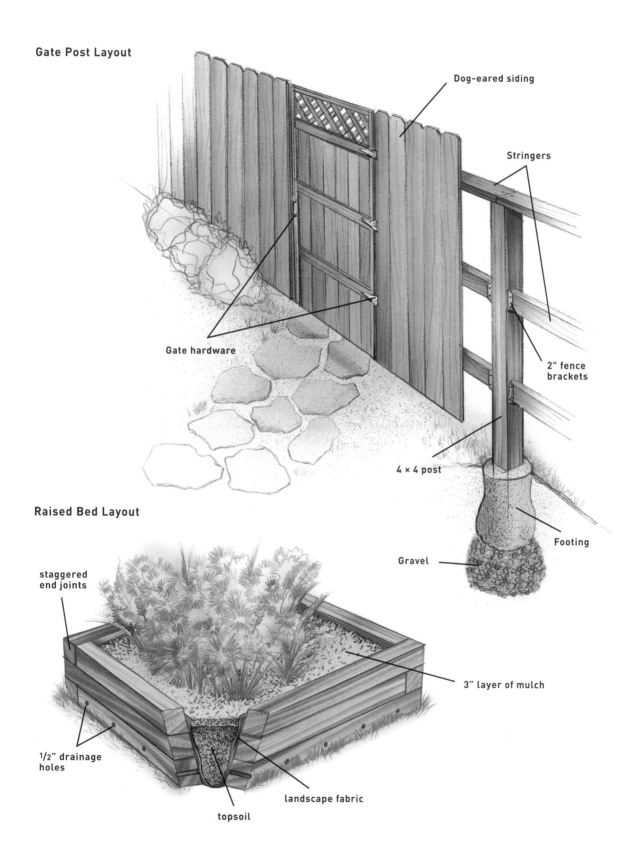

Gate Post Layout

Dog-eared siding

Stringers

2" fence brackets

Gate hardware

4 × 4 post

Footing

Gravel

Raised Bed Layout

staggered end joints

3" layer of mulch

1/2" drainage holes

landscape fabric

topsoil

Your Attic

See logbook pages 66–67

An attic is often a forgotten space, but one that serves as the lungs for a house and an early alarm for roof problems. Your interior inspection should begin with the attic. If you're like most homeowners, your attic is a dumping ground for everything that can't reasonably be stored elsewhere. Proper inspection means moving boxes as necessary to check all surfaces.

1. **Vents.** First determine how your roof is ventilated, and then ensure that vents aren't blocked and air is moving freely. There will be some combination of soffit, gable-end, and roof vents. Regardless, air should move upward. If the channels between rafters are insulated, the insulation should not be stapled or otherwise attached directly to the underside of the roof. Instead, there should be a baffle between insulation and the subroof. **Look for:** improper insulation in rafter channels; missing vent screens; vents blocked by drywall, boxes, or insulation.

2. **Subroof.** Ideally, check your attic on a sunny day and again on a rainy day. At the very least, check it on a sunny day. **Look for:** light leaks that indicate a hole or gap in roofing materials; condensation; water stain; dry or wet rot, or swelling of the subroof plywood.

3. **Structural members.** Rafters, trusses, and beams must be sound and in excellent shape. **Look for:** bowing or cracking; insect damage—especially termite tubes or sign of holes and sawdust; wet or dry rot.

4. **Insulation.** Insulation is often installed incorrectly, or the wrong insulation has been used. Unless you're familiar with

proper insulation installation, consult a professional to make sure insulation has been installed correctly and the correct insulation was used. **Look for:** missing insulation batts or empty rafter channels or joist cavities; batts with the wrong side out.

5. **Pests.** Attics are favorite nesting places for bats, raccoons, squirrels, wasps, and other rodents, insects, and animals. **Look for:** scat; animals or rodents present; obvious nests; gnawed or clawed surfaces.

Your Walls, Ceilings & Trim

See logbook pages 68–71

Homeowners see their walls and ceilings every day, but rarely take a close look. Walls and ceilings are simple structural elements, but they tell a story about what lies behind. They are also critical in the overall impression of the interior.

Check these surfaces as you work down from the attic, and forward from the back of the house. Inspect with blinds or drapes open and with a flashlight in darker areas.

- **Walls.** Check both the wall itself and any wall covering. **Look for:** buckling or bulging; water stains or damage; small holes or gnaw marks; cracking or rotting in wood paneling; peeling or wrinkled wallpaper; wallpaper seams separating; cracked or missing wall tile; cracked or deteriorated grout lines in wall tile; drywall nail "pops"; settling cracks in drywall. There are many simple wall details that will be helpful to document—just keeping track of paint manufacturers and paint color codes, or wallpaper patterns, can eliminate a lot of maddening problems should you ever need to repair walls at a later date.

- **Ceilings.** The most common problem with ceilings is water damage, but homes dating from the 1960s may include ceiling tiles or coatings that contain toxic asbestos (such as "popcorn" texturing). If you have any doubts about your ceiling surface, have it tested. **Look for:** water stains or other damage; drywall nail "pops"; settling cracks in drywall; toxic materials; buckling or bulging; cracking or rotting in wood paneling; crumbling plasterwork.

- **Trim.** The most common problem with trim is when it loosens or gets damaged, but it is often just replaced for aesthetic reasons; just replacing it with a new style can make a radical difference in a home's appearance. It is one of the most cost-effective cosmetic changes you can make to a home. Inspecting woodwork is really just a matter of looking for signs that it has loosened and checking the condition of the paintwork or stain periodically. It is a highly visible feature of your walls and ceilings, though, so regular inspection and repairs are a good idea. You may want to keep in your files the names of a couple of dependable finish carpenters who can make good repairs.

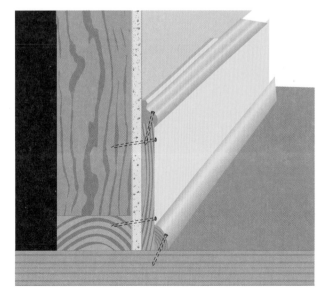

Your Foundation

See logbook page 58

Any home's foundation is the first domino in a line when it comes to potential structural problems. Small deficiencies are to be expected; foundations negotiate the difference between the house's static structure and ever-changing soil and rock.

Inspect both inside and outside your foundation. If crawling under the home is out of the question, hire somebody to check a crawlspace for you. Problems with a foundation can also make themselves known in other areas, such as doors that skewed in their openings or windows that don't open or close properly. Start by determining the type of foundation.

1. **Slab.** This is just a concrete slab on which the rest of the house is built. The enemy of all slab foundations is soil movement. If it has not been laid deep enough or with the proper base, a slab can heave and even crack. **Look for:** major cracks in the slab; slab noticeably out of level; spalling or pieces of concrete breaking off at corners or edges.

2. **Perimeter wall.** As the name implies, the home rests on walls standing on wider concrete footings. Perimeter walls can be constructed of concrete poured into forms, or built up of concrete blocks. A few newer homes user perimeter walls built of structural insulated panels (SIPs), with wood surfaces. In any case, small cracks are considered normal. Cracks larger than $1/8$ inch wide require professional attention. **Look for:** buckling or bulging of the wall (requiring immediate attention); large cracks or holes; signs of animal tunneling under walls; mud tunnels about the size of a pencil or a cigar (termite invasion); walls not plumb.

3. **Post-and-pier.** Usually only used in warm-weather climates or in areas near a body of water, where the soil is inherently less stable. The house is supported by thick posts that sit on top of concrete piers. This type is designed to accommodate more than normal soil movement. **Look for:** split or cracking posts; bowed or skewed posts; missing posts; deteriorated concrete footings.

4. **Drain tile & sump pump.** Many homes, especially in areas with high water tables or where there is rainy weather or where rain runoff is an issue, may have a system of porous drain tile imbedded in the floor around the perimeter of a basement. This drain tile system feeds into a pit served by a sump pump that activates automatically when water collects in the pit and pumps water away from the house, thereby preventing basement flooding. Sump pumps do not last forever, and therefore should be inspected periodically and replaced when they show signs of failing.

Your Flooring

See logbook pages 72–73

Flooring is second only to walls in terms of surface area, so it makes a big impact on a home's appearance. It's also a safety issue. Deteriorated floor surfaces can be tripping hazards—a serious consideration if the home has elderly occupants or anyone with mobility difficulties. Kitchen and bathroom flooring must be watertight to avoid substructure damage.

Check all flooring during your inspection and note problems as you find them. In most cases, replace or upgrade floor surfaces as budget and time allow. Some repairs, such as regrouting failing older tile, should be done immediately.

1. **Carpeting.** Carpet can harbor allergens and lower indoor air quality, so regular cleaning is a must. Any regular cleaning loosens fibers and ages the carpet. **Look for:** intractable stains; show-through of tack strips (the strips that hold the carpet in place); balding patches; pull-away from tacking along walls and seams; water stains.

2. **Wood.** Wood flooring is some of the most beautiful and durable. **Look for:** deep scratches or scuffs; cracking planks or strips; popped or missing strips or planks; warping or moisture-related problems; discoloration; worn finish.

3. **Resilient.** This broad category includes both sheet and tile products, in vinyl, linoleum, laminate, and marmoleum. **Look for:** cracks, punctures, and tears; separation at seams; wearing away of surface finish or image; fading; peeling away from the subfloor.

4. **Tile.** Tile is some of the most durable flooring, offering an incredible variety of looks. Ceramic, glass, and porcelain tile are most susceptible to breakage, and the Achilles' heel of all tile are grout lines. **Look for:** broken or "popped" tiles; grout lines that absorb water; cracked or crumbling grout; visibly discolored grout; cracked, separating, or missing caulk between tile floors and fixtures such as tubs.

Your Home's Systems

Running throughout your home's structure, and affected by and affecting that structure, are several complex systems. These make the house more livable. They include the electrical system, water service and plumbing, and heating, ventilation, and air-conditioning (HVAC). Some homes also have a security system tied into the electrical (and sometimes HVAC) system, and connected to the structure at critical access points. Any home's systems are prone to a variety of problems and require ongoing maintenance. Fortunately, most of that maintenance doesn't require extensive knowledge.

This section begins with your electrical system, your home's nervous system. It is interlinked with the HVAC and plumbing

systems. Although the techniques described are basic and straightforward, if you fear electricity or are concerned about old wiring and fixtures in your home, hire an electrician for this part of the inspection.

The section concludes with an overview of electronic home monitoring and automation systems. These are becoming increasingly more prevalent as the technology becomes cheaper and easier to use. You don't have to automate your whole house to take advantage of technology—you can adapt one piece at a time.

Your Electrical System

 See logbook pages 74–75

Unless your electricity is supplied through underground wires, it will come in via wires strung from overhead poles to a "weather head," a pole with a rounded top cap and rubber gasket through which the main power lines to the house run. The weather head connects to your electrical meter through a pipe called a "mast." Both the weather head and the mast protect power lines from the elements—most importantly, from water. The weather head, wiring, and mast are the homeowner's responsibility. Although you should regularly inspect the weather head and mast, never touch either one or the power lines. Any problems require a licensed and insured professional electrician.

The service wires will then run to an electrical meter, usually mounted outside the home or in a garage. In older models, the electrical meter is an analog model with rotating dials, which for billing purposes is "read" by a utility employee who visits your home; but newer electrical meters are digital, and may be read by transponders that send signals wirelessly.

- **Weather head and mast. Look for:** cracks; separation between head and mast; missing or damaged gasket; separation between mast and meter box; a mast or head that is not plumb; missing weather head.
- **Service wires.** Lines coming from the pole are the power utility's responsibility, but you should still check the lines and the weather head connection. **Look for:** breaks in power line sheathing; lines without a dip or loop before the head (which stops water from dripping along the line into the head); crossed or touching lines or connection; missing, corroded, or

damaged connectors; trees with branches that threaten or rub against the service wires.
- **Electrical meter.** There's not much you're allowed to do with an electrical meter, and not much to watch out for, except: mounting brackets that are loose or detached; cracked enclosure or fogged glass or digital windows.

PROFESSIONAL INSPECTION SCHEDULE

Experts recommend having a licensed electrician conduct a thorough electrical system inspection in the following circumstances: home is more than 40 years old; a major appliance has recently been added; the home has undergone a major renovation.

MONEY WATCH

Utilities across the country are beginning to offer "smart meters" to their customers. These monitor household usage and can shut down appliances at periods of peak demand, lessening power grid load. The payoff is that the utility bills electricity at lower-than-peak rates, potentially saving you hundreds of dollars a year. To learn more, contact your local utility.

The traditional analog electrical meter (left), is slowly being replaced by the digital version (right).

27

Your Breaker Panel or Fuse Box

See logbook pages 74-75

A breaker box—or fuse box in older homes—routes electricity from the main service wires coming into the house to different household circuits. Each circuit serves a different part of the house, powering fixtures, outlets, appliances, and mechanical systems, like the furnace and air conditioner. Breakers control and send power to the circuits (or a fuse, in the case of a fuse box), and protect the circuit wires and fixtures. When a circuit overloads or surges, the breaker "trips" or the fuse blows, thereby preventing them from melting and potentially causing fires. The breaker box (right) is often located with the main power shut-off, although it is sometimes outside, near the meter. Breaker boxes in newer houses have between 20 and 40 circuits. Older fuse boxes (below) may have as few as 6. More is usually better.

Newer, larger (2,000-square-feet or more) houses may have 200-amp service, while 150-amp service is common. Older and smaller homes may have 100-amp service or even less. Note the amperage if not already listed on the box—this will be crucial for any electrician working on the system.

You also need a map of your circuits, so that you can shut down parts of the system as need be. If your circuit panel or fuse box doesn't have an attached map, use the form found in the logbook section to create one.

Breaker/fuse box. As one of the most potentially dangerous areas in the home, the breaker box must be kept in good working order. **Look for:** stains or water damage around the box; scorch marks near breakers or fuse receptacles; loose clamps or wires; missing cover; loose fasteners holding the box to the wall.

BE SAFE! THE ELECTRICAL SAFETY CHECK

The best rule of thumb is to always call a licensed electrician to inspect or handle any aspect of your home wiring system. If you chose to do any of this yourself, before locating and inspecting parts of your home's electrical system, make sure you're clear about proper safety procedures, and don't do it at all if you are uncertain about these practices. The rules below should be followed any time you deal with an electrical appliance, equipment, an outlet, or a fixture. Here are some of the rules electricians use when inspecting a wiring system:

- Remove metal jewelry and make sure your hands are dry. Also make sure that floors and walls are free of moisture— sometimes an issue in basements.

- Wear rubber-soled shoes or boots. The insulating quality of rubber will prevent them from transmitting electrical current.

- Treat all circuits, fixtures, and electrical equipment as if they are live. Electricians always test circuits and verify they have been turned off before doing any work.

- Use tools with non-conductive handles (i.e., rubber coated).

- Never modify the plug on an electrical cord or extension cord.

- Do not overload a single extension cord with several appliances.

- Do not use tools, appliances, or other devices that exceed the ratings of the outlets they are plugged into or the circuits feeding those outlets.

- Light bulbs should not exceed the wattage ratings of the light fixtures that hold them.

- Use the appropriate extension cord length for the purpose, and make sure it is of sufficient "gauge" to handle the load. The packaging on extension cords will indicate the purposes for which they are suited.

- Discard and replace frayed or damaged electrical cords or extension cords.

- Do not run electrical or extension cords across door thresholds or under rugs or radiators.

- If you need to change a fuse or flip a breaker, do so with one hand (put the other hand in your back pocket). This ensures that you don't complete a circuit across the panel.

- Never stand near water or moisture when working on an electrical appliance, fixture, outlet, or electrical box.

- Any equipment, appliance, or light fixture that produces a zap or tingle when touched should immediately be disconnected and repaired or replaced.

- Do not store flammable liquids, such as paints, paint solvents, kerosene, or other fuels, near the circuit breaker box or anywhere close to electrical equipment or fixtures.

- If an outlet or switch feels warm to the touch, or you frequently blow the fuse on a given circuit and the lights on that circuit regularly flicker, call a licensed and insured electrician.

Your Wiring

Leading out from the individual circuit breakers or fuses, each branch circuit in your house carries current outward to various outlets, light fixtures, or appliances through a system of metal wires. Usually (and virtually always in home built after 1965) these circuit wires will be in the form of individual insulated wires sheathed inside a vinyl outer casing—a type of cable known as NM. However, in older homes, and in some applications in exposed utility areas, the wiring will be contained in metal or plastic conduits. And in very old homes that have not been updated, the wiring might even now consist of wires insulated in rubber and cloth and mounted in ceramic channels and brackets—a system usually called "knob and tube."

It is not unusual for homeowners to not even know what kind of wiring they have, because the wires are largely hidden behind finished walls, ceilings, and floors. However, you may get some hint during times when you're repairing walls and floors, or by looking at the wires where they immediately leave the fuse panel. And it's a good idea to learn what kind of wiring you have, or to verify it when you are shopping for a new house. Newer NM cable wiring is usually quite trouble free, while older knob-and-tube wiring will almost certainly need to be addressed and upgraded at some point.

Typically there is not much you can do yourself regarding the system wiring itself—other than spot problems and call a licensed electrician to deal with it. But here are some things to watch for:

- A circuit breaker that frequently trips or a fuse that frequently blows out. This is the sign of a damaged wire or loose connection in the circuit, a problem that needs immediate attention.
- Sheathing on cable that is cracked or brittle, or which does not properly enclose the wires inside. If you spot this, have an electrician deal with it.
- Cable or wires that are hanging loose, or which are not securely anchored to electrical boxes. This always poses potential danger and should be addressed.
- Wires that are undersized for the amperage of the circuits feeding them. This isn't always easy to determine, but the wire gauges are stamped on the vinyl casing of NM cable. Comparing what you find here with the amperage ratings on the circuit breakers can tell you if the wire gauge is proper for the circuit.
- Any knob-and-tube wiring found anywhere in your house. It is not uncommon for a home to have a combination of wiring, and while some knob and tube may be perfectly safe, it should be inspected by an electrician to verify this fact.

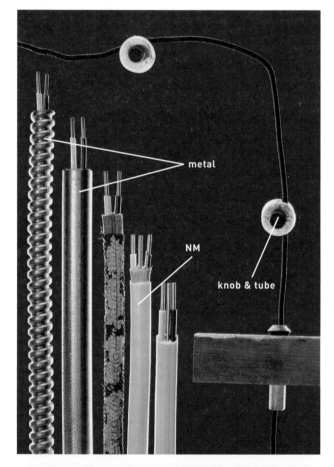

metal

NM

knob & tube

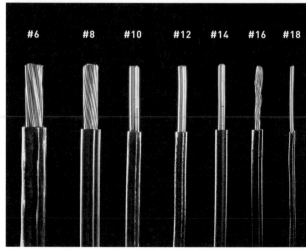

#6   #8   #10   #12   #14   #16   #18

Your Receptacles & Fixtures

 See logbook pages 76–77

Along the route of each electrical circuit are the outlets (properly called receptacles), the light fixtures, and appliances that use the electrical current in the circuits to do their work. As with any other element of your home, it's a good idea to document details like the make and model number of those features and to periodically inspect them for problems.

Start by identifying any dead outlets. Fix them immediately. Then check for any overloaded circuit or wiring issues. This is also a good time to determine if you have the appropriate number and type of outlets. Special outlets called ground fault circuit interrupters (GFCI) are used wherever moisture is an issue. Current codes call for GFCI to be installed in kitchens and baths. Many homes predate these codes, but it's wise to update outlets to GFCI where appropriate. Tamper resistant receptacles (TRR) are used in homes with small children. They have gates blocking the holes. TRRs are used in new home construction, but you should convert standard outlets to TRRs throughout the house if you have small children present.

- **Receptacles.** Check with a receptacle tester or circuit tester. **Look for:** warmth coming off the outlet; cracked or missing plastic cover plate; sparks when tester is inserted or removed; burn marks; loose outlet; dead outlet.
- **GFCI.** Inspecting GFCI means testing them:
  1. Push the "RESET" button.
  2. Plug in a tester or nightlight. The light should be on.
  3. Press the "TEST" button. The light should go out.
  4. Press the RESET button again. The light should come on.
  Look for: a failed test; burn marks; cracks; loose outlet.
- **TRR.** (photo, right) **Look for:** hole gates that open without pressure on both sides; gates stuck open or closed; missing gates; outlet hot to the touch; dead outlet.
- **Exterior receptacles.** Outside outlets must be rated for exterior use and, in most circumstances, must be covered with a metal plate. **Look for:** exposed wiring; gap in seam between conduit and receptacle box; missing faceplate; dead outlet.
- **Incandescent lights.** Check that the bulbs in each fixture don't exceed the maximum wattage for the fixture. Remove the bulbs to check the sockets. Never assume a fixture is dead because a bulb doesn't light. A burning smell requires immediate repair or replacement. **Look for:** scorch marks; fixture not adequately secured to its mounting; flickering; worn fixture finish; recessed fixtures giving off noticeable heat.
- **Fluorescent lights.** Most home lighting fixtures are incandescent or halogen, but some are older fluorescent tube

fixtures. These contain several parts that can fail, creating symptoms best diagnosed with your eyes and ears. **Look for:** consistent flickering; buzzing; hot tar smell (bad ballast).

A receptacle tester is an inexpensive tool that allows you to quickly and easily check if an electrical receptacle is live and wired correctly.

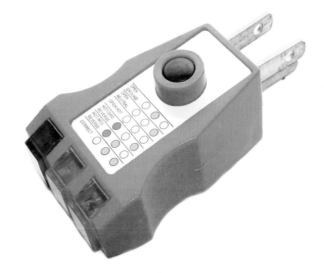

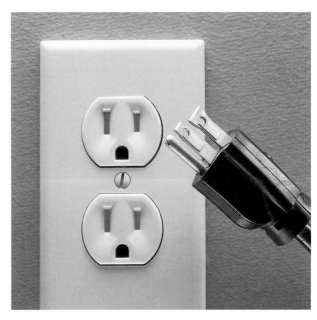

Your Water Supply System

See logbook pages 78–79

Residential plumbing only has two goals: deliver clean water and remove wastewater. To achieve those, the system is pressurized and equipped with drains and vents that equalize pressure, which in turn keep everything flowing as it should. Some water must also be heated, so a water heater is integrated into the system. On the pages that follow, we'll trace the route of that freshwater supply as it comes in from the source, moves to sinks and fixtures, then enters the drain system and exists your home.

In inspecting the system, it's important to find even small leaks. Unchecked, they can lead to thousands of dollars in damage. Be aware, also, that plumbing materials and fixtures have changed radically over time. New safety features have been developed, and more efficient fixtures have been introduced in response to an ongoing concern about water usage and conservation. Note older pipes and fixtures that you might want to replace to make the system more efficient.

If you have special concerns, such as large, old-growth trees near sewer or supply lines, you can exploit state-of-the-art technology in your inspection. A specially trained technician can perform a "camera inspection," running a flexible camera-tipped rod into the pipes. The high-resolution video camera records the entire length of underground pipes (or those encased in cement or trapped in walls), so that the technician can find even small leaks or potential blockages. The camera can reveal other issues as well, from small holes, breaks, pipe misalignments, to jewelry lost down household drains.

Start by determining where the water comes into your house. From there, cast a critical eye on your pipes, fixtures, and essential appliances—most notably, the water heater.

In some homes, particularly in rural areas, freshwater is not delivered by municipal water mains but through a well that pumps water up from groundwater supplies. Regardless of the type of pump or equipment, any well is drilled down below the local water table. The pump draws water up and into a storage tank. As the tank fills, pressure increases. When the pressure hits a preset point, the pump shuts off. When the pressure drops again, the pump turns on.

The two areas of concern are the mechanical equipment and quality of the water. Ground water can become contaminated in a variety of ways, but any contamination needs to be rectified immediately.

- **Well pump.** The two types of pumps are jet and submersible. (Jet pumps in deeper wells may be submerged, but they aren't true submersibles.) **Look for:** pumps turning on and off far too frequently; extremely noisy pump; clanking or other unusual noise.
- **Storage tank.** These are simple containers. **Look for:** rust, holes, separating seams; leakage; water or rust stains.
- **Water.** The water should be clear and odorless. However, a yearly test is recommended by the National Ground Water Association (see Resources on page 128). There are several test kits available. Use one that involves sending a sample to a lab. **Look for:** cracked or broken well head cap; construction or other surface change locally that would lead to contamination; cloudy water.

Water conservation is a pressing concern for communities across the country, and especially those in the West. Homeowners in these areas face higher water bills and periodic water-use restrictions. That makes keeping an eye on your water usage a matter of money.

Depending on your municipality, you'll be charged for every 100 cubic feet or 1,000 gallons of water (1 cubic foot = 7.48 gallons / 100 cubic feet = 748 gallons). Usage is measured by your water meter.

Your meter will be one of two types.

- "Round-reading" meters are older and less common. They feature four to six dials, with every other dial running counterclockwise.
- "Straight-reading" meters are more common. The meter includes a dial and individual number readouts. Most also include a flow indicator. If the flow indicator is spinning, water is moving through the system. If all your taps, spigots, and fixtures are turned off, a spinning flow indicator is a sign of a leak.

Water meters are sometimes located in small pits at or near the curb with a removable cover.

Your Water Treatment Systems

See logbook page 80

Whether your water comes from a well or municipal aquifer, almost all water is contaminated to one degree or another. It's just a fact of nature that water is fluid and accessible to everything from simple soil minerals to various toxic substances like fertilizers from agricultural operations, chemical waste from industry, and biological contaminates from animal and human sewage waste. Water authorities usually treat the water that passes through the system with chemicals and filters. The problem is, no single treatment or filter type removes all potential contaminants. And in some areas, water can absorb simple soil mineral substances to such a degree that they may be bitter to the taste and may cause damage to pipes and fixtures unless they are "softened" to remove these substances.

As for toxic substances, whole house filtration systems aren't perfect, but they are a step in the right direction. Typically, the water filtration system will be found along the main water supply line near where it enters the house. Whatever type of whole-house system you have, it will require periodic inspection and maintenance. For most, this means shutting off the water valves on either side of the filter, changing filters of one type or another, lubricating O-rings in some cases, checking for line clogs and—in the case of a UV filter—replacing a light bulb. Without the periodic upkeep, you might as well not have the filter. Clogged filters can also cause system-wide problems.

- **Absorption.** An absorption filter uses a medium such as activated carbon to remove contaminants. Some units use more than one media to collect a wider range of contaminants, but none trap biological pollutants. **Look for:** dirty filter indicator; leaks around the filter fittings.
- **UV.** This filter uses concentrated ultraviolet light to destroy waterborne microorganisms or pathogens. A cartridge filter catches large particulates but does not remove chemicals or fine particulates. **Look for:** burned-out bulb; leaks around the filter fittings; dirty or clogged filter cartridge.
- **Point-of-use.** Point-of-use filters can be cartridge or reverse osmosis (using a membrane as a filter). They complement whole-house filters by trapping smaller particulates and other contaminants at the source where water is consumed. **Look for:** dirty filter indicator.
- **Water softener.** If you draw your water from a well, or if your municipal water utility does not soften the water it supplies, you'll need to soften water. Chances are that your home is already equipped with a water softener.

  Water softeners trade sodium for minerals, in a process called "ion exchange." Hard water enters a "mineral tank" filled with resin beads (photo, above). Calcium and magnesium

are attracted to the beads and are then flushed off them— effectively softening the water—with the introduction of sodium chloride (otherwise known as rock salt) from the brine tank. The system is controlled with a regulator or timer, which determines when the sodium is introduced.

  Regularly testing the water will ensure that the system is working as it should. Water hardness tests are widely available. The system itself should also be regularly checked and serviced by a professional.

- **Mineral/resin tank.** These last, on average, 10 to 15 years. **Look for:** cracking or structural defects; hard water unchanged after flowing through the tank.
- **Piping/valve.** The piping into and out of the mineral tank—and between the mineral tank and brine tank—is subjected to the same failures any other plumbing pipe is. The valve allows you to bypass the system entirely and should be opened and closed once a month to keep the O-rings supple. **Look for:** corroded pipes; leaking joints or seams; leaking from the valve; stuck valve.
- **Brine tank.** This is basically just a plumbed barrel filled with salt. **Look for:** low salt level; leaks; salt crusting on the bottom.
- **Computer/clock.** Depending on the softener you own, it may have a computer to regulate tank function, or a simple clock-operated valve system. **Look for:** incorrect clock setting; error message or code; periodic shutdown; complete failure or shutdown.

Your Water Heater

See logbook page 80

Hot water on demand for a shower, bath, and washing dishes is a luxury that homeowners all too often take for granted . . . until there is no hot water. To head off that problem, you need to know what type of water heater you have, what type of fuel it uses, and more. Start with location. Water heaters are often installed in the basement or in the garage in single-level homes. Sometimes they are placed in a utility closet.

The two most common types are conventional storage tank heaters and tankless versions. Hybrid heaters are cutting edge, sold as turnkey units or as retrofits to standard tank units. They draw heat out of the air and use it to heat the water, greatly increasingly efficiency. Water heaters can be powered by gas or electricity (all hybrids are electric). Gas models cost more to buy and less to operate, but they require venting. Electric units heat the water very quickly and are easier to maintain.

1. **Conventional tank.** Tank capacity should match the number of people living in the house. If that number has increased since the unit was installed, the heater may struggle to accommodate the increased load. **Look for:** no hot water (circuit breaker); hot water that runs out (thermostat); noisy heater element; bad smell (flush the heater); leaking pressure relief valve; non-functioning pressure relief valve; water on or under the tank; dark or rusty water; sulfur odor; water always too hot or too cold (thermostat).

2. **Tankless (on-demand).** A tankless heater has to be carefully chosen to match maximum hot water needs at any given point. In the best case, these are extremely low-maintenance. They are computer controlled and will alert you to problems. That said, it's important to address even small problems quickly to avoid extremely costly repairs. **Look for:** low hot water flow; variations in temperature while the hot water is running; sulfur odor; water not hot enough (thermostat); scale/mineral build-up indicator light on; no hot water.

3. **Hybrid.** Hybrid water heaters are a conventional storage tank heater with an integrated heat pump that draws heat out of ambient air, heating water in the tank more efficiently. Inspecting the unit is similar to checking a conventional tank water heater. **Look for:** pump functioning according to manufacturer's specifications; no hot water (circuit breaker); hot water that runs out (thermostat); noisy heater element; bad smell (flush the heater); leaking pressure relief valve; non-functioning pressure relief valve; water on or under the tank; dark or rusty water; sulfur odor; water always too hot or too cold (thermostat).

BE SAFE!
Electric water heaters are high-voltage appliances—usually using a dedicated 240-volt outlet. Exercise extreme caution when attempting maintenance, a repair, or even an inspection of one of these units. If you're not comfortable working around powerful electrical circuits, call in a pro.

Your Pipes

As with electrical wires, the plumbing pipes in your house will be largely hidden behind finished walls and ceilings, and as with the electrical system, the plumbing pipes can be made of a variety of materials, and the system may be a combination of things, old and new. The best place to identify what your plumbing supply pipes and drain pipe system is made of is by looking in an unfinished utility area where wall and ceilings may be unfinished, such as in a basement, utility room, or possibly an attached garage, where the pipes will be visible.

While the pipes may be made of different materials, a plumbing system in good working order will always have the same virtues: the pipes and fitting will be secure and will not allow any water to leak.

The water supply system consists of rather narrow pipes, 1 inch or less in diameter that carries water under pressure. They are the pipes that get the most wear and tear, and the ones that should be inspected most diligently. In older homes, they are often made from galvanized iron, which has a limited life span, and should be inspected with diligence regularly—eventually they will rust through and fail. Pipes in newer houses, including many constructed right up to the present day, are made from copper—a very durable material that can give many, many decades of trouble-free service. Another material used in modern construction is a plastic pipe known as CPVC, which can also be a very durable material if installed competently. Because it is a favorite of DIYer's, though, it may be a sign that your plumbing was installed or repaired by an amateur, so inspect it carefully. Finally, a new high-end plumbing pipe is flexible PEX tubing, now approved for use in most residential plumbing codes. Thus far, it appears to be a very durable, good material for plumbing supply pipes.

Whatever your material, **look for:** seeping joints where pipes are fitted together; rusted or corroded spots in metal pipes; any cracks or bends in metal pipes; areas where plastic pipes may be rubbing against framing members and beginning to wear through.

The other piping system in your home will be large diameter branch drains and main drains. These pipes will be one and a half to six inches in diameter, and they, too, can be made from a variety of metal or plastic materials. Less susceptible to severe problems because they are under no pressure, the drain pipes should also be inspected periodically for leaks. The most common areas for trouble: seals beneath a toilet, joints beneath sinks; main drain lines. Metal pipes, usually galvanized iron or cast iron, can also be susceptible to corrosion over time.

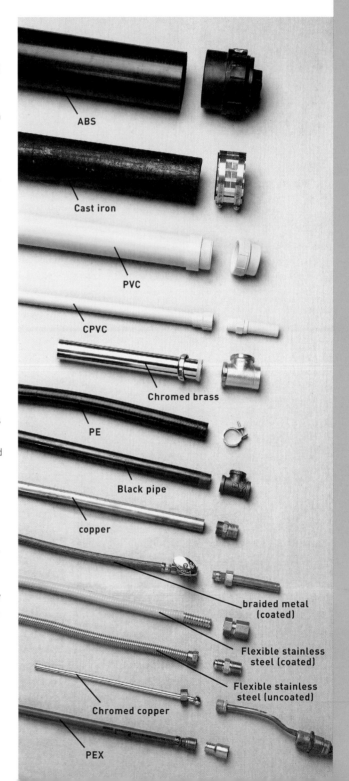

ABS

Cast iron

PVC

CPVC

Chromed brass

PE

Black pipe

copper

braided metal (coated)

Flexible stainless steel (coated)

Flexible stainless steel (uncoated)

Chromed copper

PEX

Your Water Supply Fixtures

 See logbook page 80

At the spot where water supply pipes provide water for use, which then becomes the wastewater that transitions to the drain pipe system, lie the various fixtures and appliances that make use of that water. Usually these fixtures will have water supply valves, supply tubes that help control the water that delivers to faucets, toilets, and other water-using fixtures and appliances. (In fact, you should note any fixtures that do not have shut-off valves and have them installed; they are an important safeguard when problems arise and you need to shut off water to make repairs and replacements.) Make sure to note the specifications of the various plumbing fixtures in your house, using the room-by-room documentation pages in the Logbook section of this book. Knowing the make and model number of your faucets and sinks and toilets can be quite helpful when problems arise and you need to make a trip to the hardware store or home center.

Toilet technology has evolved in response to growing need for water conservation. Low-flow toilets that use less than 1.6 gallons of water per flush are now mandated across the country. Unfortunately, many toilets were installed prior to these regulations. Older units use as much as 6 gallons per flush, and may have small, hard-to-detect leaks that waste even more water.

Although an increasing number of toilets are equipped with pressurized-valve flushing mechanisms, most still use a float mechanism—either a ball or a cup—connected to a flapper valve. Check flapper valves first, because they wear out and often settle improperly in their seat, allowing leakage. Also check the wear on the plastic bolts and mounting assembly for the seat. Given the amount of time people spend on a toilet seat, it makes sense to ensure comfort.

- **Toilet tank.** Remove the lid and check inside for cracks and other problems.
- **Bowl.** Flush and watch the action of the water. **Look for:** irregular water pattern—a sign of clogged inlet holes; iron stains; gurgling as water leaves the bowl.

There are many different types of faucets, but all can wear and deteriorate. **Look for:** leaking in a single-handle faucet in one position; constant leaking; cracks or excessive wear in the body; handle squeaking.

- **Showerheads.** Showerheads, like faucets, are usually replaced when they are more than five years old. It's a chance to upgrade to a more luxurious or water-conserving unit. However, faltering showerheads can often be brought back to life with a long bath in vinegar, which dissolves scale buildup. **Look for:** slow flow; spitting or irregular spray; leaking from wall stem or hose attachment; cracking in the head body.

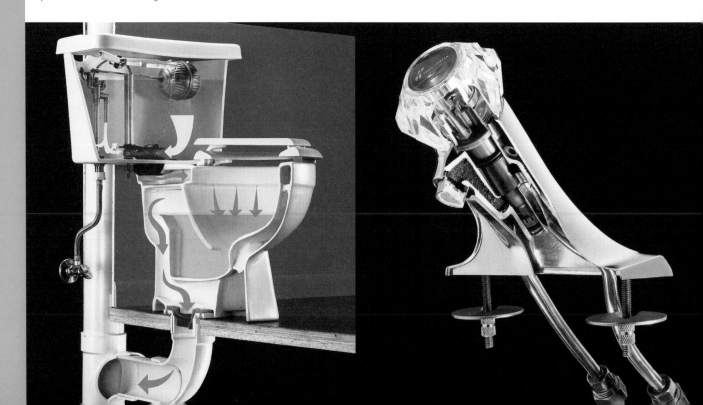

Your Sewer or Septic System

See logbook page 81

Wastewater is removed through the drain-waste-vent system—the other half of your plumbing system—through fixture drain pipes to main drain stacks and away from your house. Where that waste goes depends on where you live. If your drain system connects to a municipal sewer system, the main lines out to the sewer mains should be inspected periodically, and scoured out by auger whenever the flow is blocked or slows down. Sewer backup can be an unpleasant and costly problem, so make sure you have contact information for sewer professionals at ready reach.

Most homes are connected to a municipal sewer system. But about 25 percent of homes in America are serviced by a septic system. If yours is one of these, you need to understand septic basics and know where the parts of your system are located.

Septic systems are surprisingly simple. Waste flows out of the house through the main waste stack and into an underground tank. Solids collect on the bottom and lighter byproducts such as grease float to the top in a scum layer. Wastewater between these two layers flows out through a baffle and is routed through a distribution box. It leaches into the ground through perforated pipes in trenches covering a drain field.

Properly maintained, the system is an invisible part of your plumbing. Follow the rules below, and have your tank pumped out and cleaned every two to three years—more often if you live in a cold climate, have a small septic system, or if more than four people live in your home.

You also need a map of the system. The septic system location is usually included in an "as built" drawing for the home. If it wasn't, or you can't locate the drawing, you can usually find a map of the field with your local zoning or building department. Failing that, any company that pumps and cleans your septic tank can provide you with a map of the septic system, including the drain field trenches and pipes.

SEPTIC SYSTEM GUIDELINES

Because they are buried, septic system parts are subject to compaction, root growth, and soil movement. It's easy to forget what's underground; keep these guidelines in mind when working in your yard.

- Never park a vehicle over the tank or drain field. This can compact the soil and create a slow-draining condition.
- Do not plant trees in or near the drain field. Even small trees will grow over time and may develop an extensive root network. Roots infiltrating drain field pipes can be a major—and expensive—problem.
- Direct gutter downspouts and basement sump pump outlets away from the drain field. Too much water creates the same conditions as compacted soil.
- Check and correct drainage. If water pools over the drain field after a hard rain, the field is not sloped enough. This problem needs to be rectified to avoid costly damage.

- **Septic tank.** Some tanks are completely buried, but most have access manhole covers and risers that indicate the tank's location. **Look for:** noxious gases escaping around the manhole cover; sewage backing up into toilets and drains; noxious gases coming from drains; gurgling toilets or gurgling in drains; slow draining.
- **Drain field pipes.** Time, soil movement, and roots can all compromise leach pipes. **Look for:** waste pools gathering at points in the drain field; boggy, sodden soil; sewage backing up into toilets and drains; noxious gases from drains; gurgling toilets or gurgling in drains; slow draining.

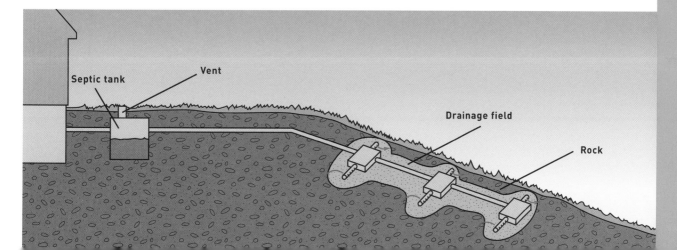

Your HVAC System

See logbook pages 84–85

HVAC stands for heating, ventilation, and cooling. The system is responsible for maintaining a comfortable home interior year-round. It involves a furnace or boiler and a variable system of ducts, pipes, radiators, or vents.

Hot water or steam systems actually have much in common with your plumbing system. Water is heated (sometimes until it forms steam—depending on the system), and then circulated via pipes to room radiators. Cooled water is routed back to the boiler to be reheated. These systems are relatively trouble-free, though the gas-fired boilers should occasionally be serviced for inspection and cleaning.

Forced-air systems use a gas or electric furnace to heat air, which is then blown into ducts that route the air throughout the house. The air flows out of vents in individual rooms. Because forced-air systems have motors and blowers, they are more likely to require service and even replacement. Make sure to have a dependable service person on file.

Central air conditioning uses an external compressor with a fan, condenser, and coils. Air is drawn into the compressor over coils containing refrigerant. The refrigerant draws heat from the air, and the cooled air is then distributed through ducts. Local air-conditioning can be installed on a room-by-room basis, using a window air conditioner or a newer "mini-split" unit, which is a hybrid of wall and central air conditioning.

Essential Ventilation. The V in HVAC is just as important as the other letters. That's because your house is meant to breathe. Move air into, up, and through the home, and you remove contaminants and moisture. Left stagnant, those can create problems ranging from mild (peeling wallpaper) to major (subsurface black mold). Proper ventilation is crucial to good indoor air quality.

Many pollutants can affect indoor air quality. Anything that burns— from cigarettes to wood stoves—creates both smoke and potentially harmful byproducts such as carbon monoxide. Artificial surface coverings from vinyl wallpaper to recycled plastic (PET) carpeting can offgas a variety of toxins for years. Even household cleaning products can create airborne allergens. When too little outdoor air is cycled into the living space, indoor airborne pollutants can become concentrated to the point of posing a health risk. In fact, EPA studies have shown that, on average, indoor quality is two to five times more polluted than outdoor air in the same area.

Outdoor air comes in through cracks and gaps, doors and windows, and by way of vent fans and other mechanical sources of ventilation.

Vent fans are used in bathrooms and kitchens and, less often, in the attic. They remove steamy air from bathrooms that can create ongoing moisture problems. A kitchen vent fan is a must for removing cooking

Boiler system

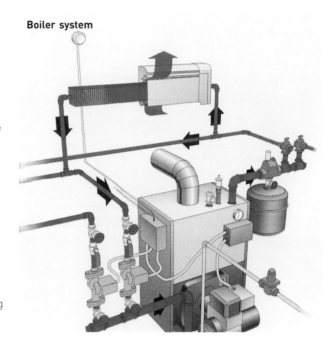

Forced air system

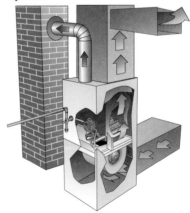

odors and ensuring airborne grease doesn't stick to walls.

Attic, or whole-house, fans draw fresh air up through the spaces below. Large, whole-house fans have largely been replaced by air conditioning. But a large, high-cfm whole-house fan can cool the entire house after the sun goes down, and do it entirely with fresh air.

Look for: blocked vents; non-functioning kitchen, bathroom, or whole-house fans; windows stuck shut; fans drawing very little air.

Your Boiler or Furnace

 See logbook page 82

The difference between a boiler and a furnace is air. A furnace heats air and blows it into ducts that distribute it throughout the house. A boiler heats water. The hot water or steam circulates through exposed pipes, baseboard heaters, or radiators.

Efficiency is a key. Furnaces are more energy-efficient than boilers. Electric units are more efficient than gas-fired models. The Federal Trade Commission (FTC) has required energy efficiency ratings on all new heating units since 1992. The ratings measure annual fuel utilization efficiency (AFUE), the percentage of fuel burned that translates directly to heat. Any post-1992 unit should have the AFUE rating marked on the cabinet.

Even without the rating, you'll find other indications of efficiency. For instance, a furnace or boiler with a continuous pilot light and a physically heavy heat exchanger will likely be low efficiency. Smaller units with electronic ignitions and smaller diameter flue will be more efficient. The most efficient have a secondary heat exchanger and sealed combustion.

Older units that are still in good shape can be retrofitted and upgraded to make them more efficient and low maintenance. You can hire an expert to perform a combustion efficiency test to determine your current model's efficiency. A furnace or boiler lasts 15 to 20 years. If yours is aging, you'll find that newer technology has advanced by leaps and bounds, and you should probably consider replacement.

1. **Forced-air furnace.** Start by determining the fuel source. Most furnaces are gas, which involves checking pilot light and vents. A clean cabinet means there is limited dirt and debris that could clog air vents. **Look for:** damaged or leaky vent or chimney connection pipe; smell of gas (heat exchangers in gas-fired furnaces mix air and gas and often leak as they age, requiring professional attention immediately); combustion chamber cracks; incorrect fuel settings and flame height and color; failed seals between furnace and ductwork; dirty furnace filter.

2. **Boiler.** Boilers—steam or hot water—are both plumbing and heating fixtures. Standing water is a sign of trouble. Check pressure-release valves on the boiler and on radiators or baseboard units. **Look for:** *hot water system*: functioning pressure-release valve; properly functioning high-level control; pressure tank filled with air, not water; dirty heat exchanger; *steam system*: sediment buildup; malfunctioning low-water cutoff safety control or high-limit safety control; float chamber sediment; dirty heat exchanger; leaks at radiator connections; pipe joint; obvious corrosion or rust.

BE SAFE!
If your furnace or boiler was installed between 1987 and 1993, and is a fan-assisted, non-condensing unit, there is a chance that it may have been vented through a horizontal, non-PVC plastic vent pipe. That type of venting was recalled and must be replaced by stainless-steel vent pipe. If you find this is how your unit is vented, contact your local utility or heating professional immediately to have the vent pipe replaced and the situation assessed for the possibility of installing a draft-inducing fan near the vent outlet to create adequate draft.

Your Air Conditioning

See logbook page 83

Not every home has air conditioning, but every home could. Your home may benefit from the luxury of a complete central air-conditioning system, be on the cutting edge with area-by-area mini-split air conditioners, or be equipped with reliable (if not very efficient) wall or window units.

All air conditioners use air filters. Filters on central-air systems and mini-splits can be either washable or replaceable. Wall and window air conditioners use washable filters. All air-conditioning filters are rated with a minimum efficiency reporting value (MERV), from 1 to 12. The higher the number, the more effective the filter, but the harder the unit will work to push air through. Weigh energy used against how dirty the local air is when choosing a replacement filter.

Proper air seals are key to avoiding energy waste. Perform a smoke test as part of your inspection. Light a punk or stick of incense and hold it near the seams between a window or wall unit and mounting sleeve or window frame (or at the joints of central-air ductwork). Smoke will reveal any air penetrating the seal. Note the area and schedule a repair.

- **Central AC.** Cools entire house, maintaining even temperatures, and highly controllable environment. Central A/C can add hundreds to your power bill. Cleaning the compressor unit helps increase efficiency and longevity. **Look for:** dirty air filter; dirty compressor/condenser unit—grill, cooling fins, fan; hose secured improperly; hose insulation degrading or falling off; insulation around ducts in attics and crawlspaces; overgrown plants or built structures intruding on necessary clearance around the condenser/compressor unit.

- **Window or wall air conditioners.** Allow you to cool a single room, but they are inefficient. Homeowners also tend to buy units too large for the square footage. If you're doing your inspection during the winter, check window or wall units wherever they are stored. Plug them in and check their operation by running them on a worktable or sawhorses. **Look for:** excessive fan noise; malfunctioning timer; unstable mounts; gaps around the window frame or sleeve and A/C unit; dirty intake fins; dirty compressor or evaporator; missing or damaged thermostat; blocked drain ports; air does not get cold.

- **Mini-split air conditioners.** A recent innovation, they are a cross between wall air conditioner and central-air system. The blower unit is mounted on a wall and coolant lines are routed out to an exterior condenser unit. These "ductless" units can last 15 years or more if properly maintained. Check the exterior compressor just as you would with a central-air system. **Look for:** dirty filter; vegetation or debris around the exterior compressor; dirty compressor; non-functioning remote.

MONEY WATCH

Bigger is not necessarily better when it comes to room air conditioners. An oversized wall or window air conditioner will waste energy. The same is true of an underpowered unit. Check room air-conditioner capacity and make sure you're using the right size units. Professionals multiply the room's square footage by 20 (the number of BTUs necessary to cool a square foot). Adjust that number based on variables that can make the room hotter or colder—such as southeast exposure or high, vaulted ceilings. Round the total number up to the next standard air-conditioner size, and that's the right unit for the room.

Window/Wall AC BTU Calculator

Room Square Footage	
BTU calculation (sq. ft x 20)	
Subtract 10% for a shaded room	
Subtotal:	
Add 10% for an extremely sunny room	
Subtotal:	
Add 10% for walls of windows	
Subtotal:	
Kitchen: add 4000 btu	
TOTAL	

BE SAFE!

Air-conditioning systems contain refrigerant—a gas sealed inside tubes that draw heat from the air passing over the tubes. Under normal operation, refrigerant will stay good for the life of the unit. If you have a leak, however, the unit will cool air less efficiently. In the event of a refrigerant leak, stop using your air conditioner until a professional addresses the problem. Never try to fix a refrigerant problem yourself; it is sealed under high pressure and the gas can be extremely dangerous.

Your Vent Fans

Used correctly, house fans can supplement your HVAC system, making it more efficient and lowering energy costs.

- **Ceiling fan.** Many ceiling fans incorporate a lighting fixture, making an inspection somewhat more complicated. This is also a chance to clean an often overlooked area. Use a stepladder to closely inspect the fan. It's the best way to see potential problems. **Look for:** wobbly blades or base; loose mounting hardware; loud noise during operation; loose connections between blades and motor rotors; speeding up and slowing down during operation; non-responsive remote control; sparking or burn marks around the base.

- **Whole-house fan.** A whole-house fan can replace air conditioning. The powerful fan draws air in through windows and up through the attic. The movement cools the air and draws in cool outside nighttime air. That can lower the interior house temperature by ten degrees or more. Inspect a whole-house fan both while it is running and when it's off. **Look for:** smoke coming from the motor (improper lubrication); squeaking drive belt; wobbling or vibrating fan blades or housing; loose mounting hardware; frayed or damaged power cord (if not hard wired); varying speed; improperly sealed cover or vent shield.

- **Bathroom fan.** Remove the screen over the fan. Silence a noisy fan with a squirt of silicone lubricating spray on the

MONEY WATCH

When inspecting your ceiling fans, measure the blade span and then check the chart below to make sure you have the correct size for the room in which the fan is located.

Ceiling Fan Size

Room Size (sq. ft.)	Fan Blade Span (in.)
0–50	30
50–100	36
100–200	42
200–350	52

moving parts. These fans can also be easily removed and replaced. If lubrication doesn't silence the fan or it just doesn't draw air the way it should, replace the fan. **Look for:** scorch marks; a slow-running fan; rust, corrosion, or moisture damage around the housing; excessively noisy fan.

- **Kitchen fan.** Most kitchen vent fans are located either in the range hood or in the wall near the stove. These normally have a filter that must be cleaned regularly, according to the manufacturer's recommendations. If the fan is vented to the outside, there must also be a cover or door to ensure the opening is sealed when the fan isn't on. **Look for:** dirty fan filter; unusually slow speed; fan opening blocked from the outside (such as with overgrown plants); sparking, scorching, or other signs of electrical short; excessive noise.

Bathroom vent fan

Your Safety & Security Systems

See logbook pages 86–87

Safety in the home is about more than just putting decals on the sliding glass door or no-slip strips in the bathtub. It's also about making sure fire doesn't get the best of you and—in an increasing number of homes—even having someone monitor your home from a distance.

The ever-growing trend toward wireless everything has had an impact on how we interact with, and secure, our homes. From smoke alarms that can detect infrared patterns to warn sleepers of a fire long before the smoke gets thick, to central-station alarm systems that can remotely unlock our doors when we forget our keys, automation and electronic innovation is changing home safety.

Of course, the vast majority of homes have more low-tech options. A strategically placed fire extinguisher, motion-detecting outdoor light, or old-school battery operated smoke detector can be a lifesaver. You can also take some simple steps to ensure your home is an unappealing target for criminals (see The Home Security Inspection Checklist, on page 87).

- **Security and alarm systems.** Any alarm system is only as good as its weakest link. Start by calling your security provider if home monitoring is part of your system. Give them your password and let them know you'll be testing the system. All security systems focus on securing the perimeter, so start by closing doors and windows and checking the security panel to see if there is a break in the perimeter "fence." Most panels will show a light if a window or door is open. It will also have a test button, and some even include a self-analysis and diagnosis feature. Consult the system's documentation. **Look for:** blinking alert light even though all openings are secured; no message sent to the central station when the perimeter is breached; self-test malfunction; missing or misaligned contacts on doors or windows.
- **Fire protection.** The first line of fire defense is working smoke alarms. It's also wise to locate several fire extinguishers throughout the house—ideally in the kitchen, garage and near sleeping areas. Use fire extinguishers labeled "ABC," because they will fight any fire, from a grease flare to an electrical fire. If you have a two-story home, consider a folding or accordion-style emergency escape ladder in every upstairs bedroom. **Look for:** working smoke alarm batteries (and replace the batteries in any case, according to the schedule

on page 86); expired smoke detectors (the United States Fire Administration recommends replacing smoke detectors at or before 10 years); working fire extinguishers; fire extinguisher gauge with needle anywhere but in the green; cracked nozzle or hose, or missing fire extinguisher pin on; blocked means of emergency egress.
- **Exterior safety and security.** Making your home as secure as possible is a matter of line of sight. If your home can be viewed clearly from many different angles, burglars are less likely to strike. Appropriate exterior lighting is essential. Exterior lights should be equipped with at least a 40-watt bulb, and there should be a light for every door. Consider upgrading to motion-detecting light fixtures. **Look for:** landscaping blocking the view into windows or entry doors; burned out exterior light bulbs; dark, shadowed areas near the house.

Section 3 Your Appliances

Large appliances are key elements to consider in any home inspection. Not only do they make a room such as a kitchen usable, they are also some of the biggest consumers of energy in the home.

Check for two issues with your appliances. First and most obvious, look for problems. Second, consider whether it would be wise to replace and/or upgrade the appliance. Both of these are matters of money.

A malfunctioning appliance, such as a leaking dishwasher or refrigerator, can potentially do hundreds—if not thousands—of dollars in damage if the problem goes undetected. Even if the problem is not that severe—a corrupt seal on the door of a stove— the cost of wasted energy could still be significant.

In addition, appliance technology is continually being refined. Depending on how old your appliance is, it may be two or three generations removed from current technology. An older gas stove may have a constantly burning pilot light rather than a more current electronic "on-demand" ignition. Your refrigerator—traditionally an energy hog—might not be an Energy Star-rated model.

The latest generation of appliances include "smart" models that contain computers and wireless connections and have the ability to monitor usage and adapt their operation accordingly. If you are a tech-savvy homeowner and comfortable with this type of technology, consider upgrading.

In any case, use the chart below to log your appliance's age and measure it against average longevity, for a snapshot of where you are in your appliances' life spans.

Appliance Longevity

Appliance	Average Life	Your Unit
Gas range	± 20	
Electric range	± 15	
Refrigerator	± 15	
Microwave	± 7	
Freezer	± 13	
Dishwasher	± 10	
Trash Compactor	± 8	
Washer	± 12	
Dryer	± 15	

Your Refrigerator/Freezer & Range/Oven

 *See logbook page 88*

Refrigerators and freezers can be the biggest consumers of electricity among appliances. Keeping yours running in top shape will translate to bottom-line energy cost savings.

Those savings can be significant. Units manufactured prior to 2001 use, on average, 40 percent more electricity than an equivalent new Energy Star model. Regardless of age, proper maintenance can save hundreds of dollars a year and will extend the refrigerator's life.

The bigger the unit, the more energy it consumes. If you are an empty nester or a small household with a large refrigerator, an inspection is the time to start assessing downsizing.

Routine scheduled maintenance on these major appliances mostly involves self-imposed tasks: inspecting and cleaning cooling coils and burner once or twice yearly, and replacing water filters for the refrigerator icemaker and water dispenser. These are among the most expensive of all home appliances, though, so make sure you keep reference information for their warranties at ready reach. Many homeowners come to understand that appliance insurance covering these major appliances is money well spent.

- **Coils.** Proper air circulation around the unit's coils ensures efficiency, as does keeping the coils clean. Refrigerator coils are either mounted on the back, or on the front at the bottom (behind a grill below the door). **Look for:** dirt, dust, and debris on coils; less than one inch clearance between wall- and back-mounted coils; damaged, crimped, or corroded coils; leaking coils (requires immediate professional attention).
- **Gaskets.** The traditional gasket test is to close the door(s) with a dollar bill between the frame and door gaskets. If the bill can be pulled out with little to no resistance, the gasket should be replaced. **Look for:** loose seals; permanently crimped or collapsed areas on the seal; dirty seals.
- **Water filter.** Automatic icemakers and water dispensers include an inline filter, which should be changed every six months. This is more about health than saving money, but is still essential. **Look for:** old water filter; ice or water from the refrigerator that tastes "off."
- **Drain.** The drain pan and the drain tube should be cleaned every six months. Flush the tube with a mixture of ammonia and warm water. **Look for:** drain pan full of dirty wastewater; mold growth in the pan or tube; clogged tube.

MONEY WATCH
Refrigerators and freezers run more efficiently when full. If your refrigerator or freezer is less than half full, place plastic gallon jugs full of water inside. Use a thermostat to check both the refrigerator and freezer temperature; ideally, the refrigerator should be kept between 36 and 40 degrees Fahrenheit, and the freezer between 0 and 3 degrees Fahrenheit.

Ranges and cooktops are either gas or electric. In either case, cleanliness is defense against potential problems.

First, determine how accurate your controls are. Set the oven to 350 degrees Fahrenehit and allow it to completely preheat. Use a quality thermometer to note the internal temperature versus the readout/set temperature: Older units can vary as much as 20 degrees. If the variation is more than 30 degrees, call a repairman or start shopping for a new oven. Note any variation in the log on page 88—this will help you adapt any recipe you cook in the meantime.

- **Gas burners.** Check burner flame color, height, and consistency. Poke the holes and scrub the burners as needed. **Look for:** uneven flame heights; orange instead of blue flame; burners that have difficulty igniting; cracked burners.
- **Door.** Slowly move your hand around the edge of the door with the stove heating. Check for hot air flowing out around the gasket. Note hot spots that have become obvious during cooking. **Look for:** heat escaping around door; hot spots front to back or side to side inside; burned-out light bulb.
- **Cleaning.** Test any self-cleaning feature (follow the manufacturer's instructions precisely), or clean the oven thoroughly. Always unplug an electric stove when cleaning it. **Look for:** damaged interior surfaces; obvious hot spots or dead spots on heating element; a self-cleaning feature that doesn't entirely clean the oven; flaking or worn paint on the interior.
- **Electric burners.** Set the burners on high. **Look for:** obvious dead spots or hot spots; burner coils that don't sit level; slow-to-heat burners.
- **Connections.** It's essential to verify the condition of hoses, cables, and connections. **Look for:** damaged or aging gas hose; sulfur odor; frayed or damaged electrical cord; scorch marks around plug.

Your Garbage Disposer & Dishwasher

See logbook page 88

A garbage disposer is a wonderful convenience that makes kitchen cleanup a breeze. That doesn't mean you can put anything down the disposer (see the rules, right). The good news is, use a modicum of common sense, and the disposer will last a good long time.

The unit is installed between the sink drain and drainpipe, and may also be plumbed to a dishwasher. It's wired to a switch; when turned on, a powerful motor in the unit spins sharp blades at high speed to process food waste into small particulates. There's a small red reset button on the underside of most disposers—the first solution you should try when the unit stops running.

- **Motor.** Any major motor problem usually translates to a new disposer. Always check the breaker powering the switch. **Look for:** stalled motor (possible jam); motor doesn't start; smoke; intermittent motor activity (possible loose wiring).
- **Plumbing. Look for:** leaking; slow or intermittent running; gurgling while the disposer is in operation; water backed up into sink; chopped kitchen waste backed up into the sink; rust or corrosion; puddle of water underneath the unit.

Dishwashers are hard-working appliances that have to keep a lot of water contained inside. Dishwasher wear and tear can lead problems both hidden and not. Catching those while they're still small concerns is the goal.

Run the dishwasher with a load of dishes. If that isn't possible, run it empty. Check carefully inside and out. Unfasten the kickplate at the bottom of the dishwasher and remove it. Use a flashlight to check the water inlet valve and drain hose connections. **Look for:** standing water inside after the unit has run through a complete cycle; malfunctioning controls; leaking door gasket; loose or cracked inlet or outlet hoses; leaks at connections between hoses and the dishwasher; unused detergent in tray; large spots or streaking on dishware and glassware; water under the dishwasher or leaking out in front; rot or moisture in wood alongside the dishwasher; clogged spray arm ports; standing food debris inside.

The garbage disposer and dishwasher are among the more short-lived of home appliances, because they are filled with moving parts and are in daily use. Keep track of warranty information, and be prepared to replace them once every 10 years at a minimum. Careful research into consumer satisfaction ratings is time well spent when shoppping for new appliances.

GARBAGE DISPOSER RULES

Do:
- Read the instructions, locate the reset button, and understand how to use it.
- Frequently add citrus peels to eliminate odors.
- Periodically grind ice to clean the blades.
- Feed food scraps slowly to avoid jams, especially starchy scraps such as potato peels.
- Cut food scraps into small chunks before grinding.

Don't:
- Grind grease or meat.
- Use drain cleaners in a disposer.
- Poke inside with utensils while it is running.
- Grind nonfood debris or waste.
- Grind coffee grounds.
- Grind large animal bones.

DISHWASHER RULES

Follow these common-sense rules to keep your dishwasher running trouble-free for as long as possible.

- **Scrape off food debris.** Big pieces of food can get caught in the filter, and may be sprayed around the inside of dishwasher.
- **Avoid overloading.** Spray from the spray arms is ineffective if it can't reach dishware surfaces.
- **Use proper settings.** If you only need a quick rinse, running the heavy duty cycle wastes water and energy, and puts additional strain on the dishwasher.
- **Run sink hot water before starting the dishwasher.** This helps avoid a cold-water primary rinse.
- **Check your water heater.** The ideal temperature for washing dishes is 125 degrees Fahrenheit. If your water heater is set lower, change the setting.

BE SAFE!

Keep your hand and any hard objects out of the disposer. If you have to retrieve something from inside the disposer, shut off the power to that part of the kitchen (or the whole kitchen) and use needlenose pliers to pull out the object.

Your Washing Machine & Dryer

See logbook page 89

A washing machine saves you trips to the laundromat, and today's models are amazingly trouble-free and reliable. With just a little care, your washing machine will give you excellent service for more than a decade.

Vibration is the enemy of washer longevity, so inspecting the washer means making sure everything has been done to limit vibration, and to make sure the unit has as firm a footing as possible.

- **Hoses.** Water supply and drain hoses are often the first things to go on a washer. In fact, manufacturers recommend replacing hoses every five years. **Look for:** cracked rubber hoses; crimped hoses; leaking hose; damaged hose-end coupling; leaking inlet or outlet on the washer; bulging or hose deformation.
- **Operation**. How well the washer works can tell you a lot about its condition. Run a small load of clothes. **Look for:** lukewarm water in hot cycles; water left in the tub; clothes that are soaking wet at the end of the cycle; excessive vibration.
- **Cabinet and tub. Look for:** sticking detergent drawer; moldy smell; digital controls that don't light; analog controls malfunctioning; door doesn't close securely; damaged cabinet from vibration and impact with walls; unit not level; tub won't spin.

Dryer quality isn't just about efficiency; it's an issue of safety. Every year dozens of people are hurt or killed and homes are lost due to fires from built-up dryer lint. That damage is all easily avoided. As part of your inspection, pull out the lint filter and clean the lint trap housing. You can do this with a vacuum equipped with a wand attachment, or a long electrostatic brush, like the ones used to clean blinds. Also clean inside the vent hose.

A dryer also needs to dry efficiently to avoid damp clothes and wasted energy. Check the heating element if there is a heating problem. Here's how to get to it:

1. Unplug the dryer and unscrew the vent clamp. Move the dryer away from the wall and consult the manual to determine heating element location.
2. Remove the access panel to reveal the heating element.
3. Locate the thermostat and disconnect the wires (if you have a continuity tester or an ohmmeter). Test the thermostat. If it registers, the heating element is not the problem. If not, replace the heating element.

- **Dryer.** Check for level and inspect the door and cabinet. **Look for:** door that doesn't seal completely; bent or damaged door; damaged cabinet; excessive vibration in operation; clothes don't completely dry; smoke or overheating; digital control readout malfunctioning; drum doesn't turn.

Section 4 — Home Logbook

Congratulations! You completed a home tour, know where the crucial parts are located, and maybe even learned something about their condition simply by looking at them as you were guided by the first sections of this book. At the very least, you surely have a better idea of just how complex your house is.

But fear not. This fourth section, the Home Logbook, will give you a convenient place to document the important information about your home—things like the date of purchase for appliances; a record of what repairs were made and when they were made; a list of the various repair people and contractors you may need to call at a moments notice; the contact information for various agencies and municipal offices that may be helpful—even the colors and patterns of the various wall and floor surfaces of your home. Pretty much all of it will be right here.

This section is very easy to use. Organized in the same way as the opening section, there will be space to document the important details about every aspect of your home, beginning with roof and foundation, and moving inward to the mechanical systems, and then to the light and plumbing fixtures, and even things like furniture and accessories. The logbook concludes with a room-by-room journal that allows you to record every additional detail you might want to remember. After the logbook section, you will find other appendices that offer even more helpful information.

Don't expect to fill in every blank line in every box on every page. You won't know the details on some things at first, but over time your logbook will flesh out and become a valuable resource that provides all the critical historical data on your home, accessible at a moment's notice.

Each logbook entry will include places to record similar details: the make and model number of systems and appliances; when they were purchased; who installed or delivered; when and why they were serviced; warranty and service contract details; help-line consumer telephone numbers and website addresses, and much more. It will also suggest recommended intervals for inspection and routine service, where applicable. Always remember that these are general suggestions. The manufacturer use and care manuals will give more precise recommendations for service intervals.

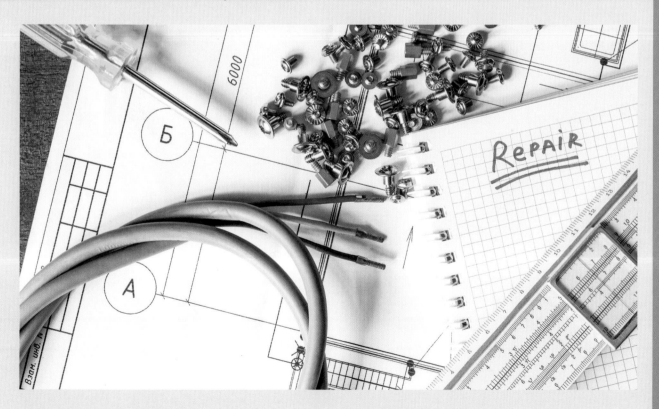

Home & Neighborhood Details ✎

Property Log

Address of property:..

Zoning:..

Legal description of property:...

Date of construction:...

Date of purchase:...

Purchase history (date and purchase price):

    First owner:..

    Second owner: ....

Number of rooms:...

Number of bedrooms:...

Number of bathrooms:..

Total square footage:...

Finished square footage:..

Lot size:...

Insurance Log

Homeowner's insurance co.: ....

Liability/damage limits:...

Insurance agent:...

    Tel:..

    Email: ....

Title insurance co.:...

Title insurance agent: ....

    Tel: ....

    Email:..

    Notes: ....

Real Estate/Financial Log

Real estate company/office:...

    Agent:...

    Tel:..

    Email: ....

Mortgage holder #1: ....

    Name of mortgage company/bank:........................

    Interest rate/length of term: ....

    Name of mortgage agent:.......................................

        Tel:..

        Email:..

Mortgage holder #2: ....

    Date of transfer: ....

    Name of mortgage company/bank:........................

    Interest rate/length of term: ....

    Name of mortgage agent:.......................................

        Tel: ....

        Email:..

Municipal Log

Police: ....

Fire department: ....

Parks and recreation board: ....

Sewer/water dept.: ....

Trash/recycling:..

Building inspection office:...

Community outreach officer: ....

Urban forestry office: ....

Construction Log

General contractor: ....

    Address:...

    Tel: ....

    Email:...

Subcontractor #1...

    Service provided: ....

    Name: ....

    Tel: ....

    Email:...

 Subcontractor #2..

    Service provided: ....

    Name: ....

    Tel: ....

    Email:...

Subcontractor #3...

    Service provided: ....

    Name: ....

    Tel: ....

    Email:...

Neighborhood Log

Name of neighborhood/borough: ....

City councilman/alderman:...

    Tel: ....

    Email:...

Crime watch number: ....

School #1...

    Main office tel:...

    Email:...

    Principal: ....

    Parent liaison: ....

    PTA:...

School #2...

    Main office tel:...

    Email:...

    Principal: ....

    Parent liaison: ....

    PTA:...

Local park:...

    Phone:..

    Email:...

    Hours of operation: ....

Notes

_____

_____

_____

_____

_____

_____

_____

The Roof 🖊 *See pages 10–11*

Roof Basics

Approximate square footage:..

Material type:...

Roofing manufacturer and style: ....

Retailer purchased from: ....

    Tel:..

    Email:...

Installation date:...

Installer:..

    Tel:..

    Email:...

Installation cost: ....

Manufacturer's warranty:...

Installer's warranty: ....

Repairs & Replacements

Date Inspected	Type of Repair

Roof Inspection Log

Date Inspected	Problems Noted

Professional Resources

#1: ....

    Tel: ....

    Email:..

#2: ....

    Tel: ....

    Email:..

#3: ....

    Tel: ....

    Email:..

Gutters, Downspouts & Vents 🖊 *See pages 12–13*

Basics

Amount of gutter trough (linear feet): ....

Number of downspouts: ....

Material type: ....

Manufacturer and style: ....

Retailer purchased from: ....

Installation date: ....

Installer: ....

    Tel: ....

    Email: ....

Installation cost: ....

Manufacturer's warranty: ....

Installer's warranty: ....

Soffit type: ....

Fascia style: ....

Professional Resources

#1: ....

    Tel: ....

    Email: ....

Gutters and Downspout Inspection Log

Date Inspected	Problems Noted

Repairs & Replacements

Date Inspected	Type of Repair

Roof Vents

	Type	Location	Date Inspected	Condition
Vent 1				
Vent 2				
Vent 3				
Vent 4				
Vent 5				

Siding ✎ *See pages 14–15*

Basics

Approximate square footage:...

Material type:...

Manufacturer & style: ....

Retailer purchased from: ....

Installation date:..

Installer:...

    Tel:..

    Email:...

Installation cost:..

Manufacturer's warranty:..

Installer's warranty: ....

Paint or Stain

Main color paint/stain brand:......................................

    Color/tint/code: ....

Trim color paint/stain brand: ....

    Color/tint/code: ....

Purchased from:..

Warranty: ....

    Applied by: ....

    Date of application: ....

Inspection Log

Date Inspected	Problems Noted

Repairs & Replacements

Date Inspected	Type of Repair

Professional Resources

#1: ....

    Tel: ....

    Email: ....

#2: ....

    Tel: ....

    Email: ....

#3: ....

    Tel: ....

    Email: ....

Notes

Windows *See pages 16–17*

Basics

Number of windows: ....

Window type #1: ....

    Manufacturer: ....

    Warranty: ....

    Date of installation: ....

    Installer: ....

Window type #2: ....

    Manufacturer: ....

    Warranty: ....

    Date of installation: ....

    Installer: ....

Window type #3: ....

    Manufacturer: ....

    Warranty: ....

    Date of installation: ....

    Installer: ....

Window Inspection Log

Date Inspected	Problems Noted

Repairs & Replacements

Date Inspected	Type of Repair

Professional Resources

#1: ....

   Tel: ....

   Email: ....

#2: ....

   Tel: ....

   Email: ....

#3: ....

   Tel: ....

   Email: ....

Window washer: ....

   Tel: ....

Glass repair/replacement: ....

   Tel: ....

Notes

_____

_____

_____

_____

_____

_____

_____

_____

_____

_____

_____

_____

Exterior Doors 🖉 *See page 16*

Basics

Number of exterior doors: ....

Entry Door #1: ....

   Manufacturer: ....

   Warranty: ....

   Date of installation: ....

   Warranty: ....

   Lockset manufacturer: ....

     Installed by: ....

Entry Door #2: ....

   Manufacturer: ....

   Warranty: ....

   Date of installation: ....

   Warranty: ....

   Lockset manufacturer: ....

     Installed by: ....

Entry Door #3: ....

   Manufacturer: ....

   Warranty: ....

   Date of installation: ....

   Warranty: ....

   Lockset manufacturer: ....

     Installed by: ....

Patio/sliding door: ....

   Manufacturer: ....

   Warranty: ....

   Date of installation: ....

   Warranty: ....

   Lockset manufacturer: ....

     Installed by: ....

Exterior Door Inspection Log

Date Inspected	Problems Noted

Professional Resources

#1: ....

   Tel: ....

   Email: ....

#2: ....

   Tel: ....

   Email: ....

#3: ....

   Tel: ....

   Email: ....

Locksmith: ....

Security company: ....

Door Repairs & Replacements

Date Inspected	Type of Repair

Garage Door Inspection Log

Date Inspected	Problems Noted

Garage Door Repairs & Replacements

Date Inspected	Type of Repair

Garage Door

Garage door:...

    Manufacturer:...

    Date of installation:...

    Installed by: ....

Garage door opener: ....

    Manufacturer:...

    Date of installation:...

    Installed by: ....

    Replacement date:..

    Make & model:...

    Replaced by: ....

    Installed by:...

Garage Door Professional Resources

#1:..

    Tel:..

    Email:..

#2:..

    Tel:..

    Email:..

#3:..

    Tel:..

    Email:..

Foundation/Foundation Walls ✏ *See page 24*

Foundation Basics

Type of foundation: ....

Year of installation: ....

Insulated? ☐ Yes ☐ No

Waterproofed? ☐ Yes ☐ No

Professional Resources

Contact: ....

    Tel: ....

    Email: ....

Contact: ....

    Tel: ....

    Email: ....

Contact: ....

    Tel: ....

    Email: ....

Sump Pump

Manufacturer: ....

Installed by: ....

Service company: ....

Sump Pump Inspection Log

Date Inspected	Problems Noted

Foundation Inspection Log

Date Inspected	Problems Noted

Repairs & Replacements

Date Inspected	Type of Repair

Walkways, Driveway & Steps ✐ *See page 18*

Driveway Basics

Material used:..

Approximate square footage:..............................

Date installed:...

    Installed by: ....

    Telephone: ....

Walkway Basics

Material used:..

Approximate square footage:..............................

Date installed:...

    Installed by: ....

    Telephone: ....

Steps Basics

Material used:..

Approximate square footage:..............................

Date installed:...

    Installed by: ....

    Telephone: ....

Professional Resources

Installation

    #1:..

    Tel: ....

Sealing/repair

    #1:..

    Tel: ....

Walkways, Driveway & Steps Inspection Log

Date Inspected	Problems Noted

Repairs & Replacements

Date Inspected	Type of Repair

Deck, Patio & Porch *See page 19*

Deck Basics

Approximate square footage:...

Material type:...

Manufacturer & style:...

Installation date:...

Installer:...

Tel:...

Website/email:..

Deck Inspection Log

Date Inspected	Problems Noted

Staining/Refinishing Log

Date	Finish Product Applied	Amount	Power Washed?

Porch Basics

Approximate square footage:...

Material type:...

Manufacturer & style:...

Installation date:...

Installer:...

Tel:...

Website/email:..

Porch Inspection Log

Date Inspected	Type of Repair

Patio Basics

Approximate square footage:...

Material type:...

Manufacturer & style: ....

Installation date:..

Installer:...

    Tel:...

    Website/email:...

Patio Inspection Log

Date Inspected	Problems Noted

Professional Resources

#1:...

    Tel: ....

    Email:...

#2:...

    Tel: ....

    Email:...

Repairs & Replacements

Date Inspected	Type of Repair

Notes

_____

_____

_____

_____

_____

_____

_____

_____

_____

_____

Landscape Features ✎ *See pages 20–21*

Fencing Basics

Approximate linear footage:...

Material type:...

Manufacturer & style: ....

Number of gates: ....

Retailer or installer: ....

Installation date:..

Installation cost:..

Fencing Repairs & Replacements

Date Inspected	Type of Repair

Professional Resources

#1:...

    Tel: ....

    Email:...

#2:...

    Tel: ....

    Email:...

Fence Inspection Log

Date Inspected	Problems Noted

Staining/Painting Log

Date	Product Used	Amount

Landscape Wall Inspection Log

Date Inspected	Problems Noted

Garden Wall Inspection Log

Date Inspected	Type of Repair

Retaining Walls

	Location	Type	Height	Drain/weep holes?
1				
2				
3				

Lawncare Basics

Lawn service company: ....

Tel: ....

Website: ....

Tree treatment & trimming: ....

Tel: ....

Website: ....

Garden service: ....

Tel: ....

Website: ....

Notes

_____

_____

_____

_____

_____

_____

_____

_____

_____

Pool & Spas

Pool/Spa Basics

Manufacturer & style: ....

Retailer purchased from: ....

Installation date:...

Installer:..

    Tel: ....

    Website/Email: ....

Daily Maintenance Checklist

Every time someone uses the pool or spa, figure on at least a small amount of cleaning and maintenance. In the height of swimming or soaking season (sometimes at opposite ends of the calendar), the following chores are often required on a daily basis:

- Remove leaves and debris from the surface of the water using a leaf skimmer (or shallow net) attached to a telescoping pole.

- Check and clean out debris from the basket for each in-wall or lily pad skimmer, the latter just under the cover mounted flush to the deck behind each skimmer location.

- Eyeball the water level of the pool or spa and refill to just above the weir line of the skimmer; during heavy or in-season use, expect more water loss from evaporation and splashing.

- Test and adjust the water quality and chemical balance (if not daily, then at least every other day during regular use).

- Run the recirculation and filtering system once every 24 hours to clean out dirt and debris and recycle the water.

Weekly Maintenance Checklist

- Hose down or sweep the pool deck, aiming away from the water's edge to keep dirt and debris from getting into the pool or spa from the wind or on the feet of swimmers and soakers.

- Gently scrub the sides and bottom of the pool or spa with a stiff-bristled brush attached to a telescoping pole, starting at the shallow end and moving from the tops of the walls with overlapping strokes and then along the bottom to direct the dirt toward the main drain in the deep end, and then into the filtration system.

- Remove any lingering dirt or debris, once settled on surfaces, by vacuuming the pool using either a unit that attaches to the skimmer to suction dirt and debris into the filtration system, or one that attaches to a garden hose to force organic matter in a collection bag (hands-free robotic pool vacuums also are available).

- Clean out the pump's strainer basket and check the condition of the pump's gasket or O-ring. Turn off power to the equipment set, lift the lid with a specially designed wrench (to avoid damage), and remove and rinse out the basket. Lubricate the gasket or, if it's already cracked or brittle, replace it with a new one.

- Check the psi (pounds per square inch) reading of the filter's pressure gauge, a measure of how many gallons per minute are running through the filter during a recirculation cycle. If it reads 10 psi higher than normal (as determined when a new/clean filter is restarted), it's likely that the filter is clogged with dirt and needs to be replaced or cleaned. A psi reading that is lower than normal indicates a clog or blockage upstream from the filter, earlier in the recirculation system.

Monthly Maintenance Checklist

- Use a stiff, nylon-bristled tile brush and specially formulated tile soap (not household cleanser) to scrub ceramic tile at the waterline, removing scale, dirt, algae growth, and other buildup.

- Shock or superchlorinate the pool water, using perhaps five times the normal amount of chlorine or sanitizer. Shocking the water kills off bacteria and algae, as well as ammonia and other chemicals and organic matter, that have accumulated as the "free" or available chlorine level has dropped.

- Drain the spa completely (usually every three to four months) using a submersible pump or manually, with buckets, cups, and sponges. Refill the vessel to the level of the highest outlet or skimmer and run fresh water through the recirculation/filtration system to flush out any remaining dirt and debris from the pipes and outlets. Drain the water and use a non-abrasive cleanser (ideally the one recommended by the spa's manufacturer or builder) to thoroughly clean the inside surfaces. Rinse off any residue (to mitigate foaming) and clean or replace the filter. Refill the spa or hot tub (the latter within two days, ideally sooner, to avoid shrinkage) and test for and adjust for water quality before using the spa.

- Use an appropriate cleaner and cleaning pad for all metal parts and accessories, including ladders, diving board frames, and handrails to mitigate corrosion.

- Backwash the filter to flush out stubborn or excessive dirt and debris, which can accumulate in systems that direct surface dirt and debris into the pool or spa's recirculation and filtration system (as opposed to removing it independently).

Notes

Attic ✐ *See page 22*

Attic Basics

Rafter structure: Traditional rafters or trusses?

    Dimensions of framing members: ....

    Spacing of framing members:...............................

Attic floor structure

    Dimensions of joists:..

    Spacing of joists: ....

Insulation, Rafters

Type:..

Thickness:...

R-value:...

Vapor barrier?...

Baffles?..

Insulation, Attic Floor

Type:..

Thickness:...

R-value:...

Vapor barrier?...

Professional Resources

#1:...

    Tel: ....

    Email:...

#2:...

    Tel: ....

    Email:...

Attic Ventilation

Type of ventilation:..

Passive gable-end vents? ☐

Ridge vents? ☐

Roof deck vents? ☐

Powered exhaust fan? ☐

Make and model: ....

    Installation date: ....

    Installed by: ....

Attic Inspection Log

Date Inspected	Problems Noted

Repairs & Maintenance

Date Inspected	Type of Repair

DIAGRAM OF ATTIC

Notes

Walls, Ceiling & Trim 🖉 *See page 23*

Note: Houses have a variety of wall and ceiling surfaces found in different locations. For example, bathroom walls might be ceramic tile; family room walls, paneling. And trim moldings may vary greatly in style and material from room to room. In this section, simply note the different types of materials your home uses in its walls and ceilings. More detailed information on the components in each room can be logged in the room-by-room log pages, found on pages 90-111.

Ceiling Surfaces

Ceiling surface #1

    Type:..

    Rooms where found: ....

    Installation date: ....

    Installed by: ....

Ceiling surface #2

    Type:..

    Rooms where found: ....

    Installation date: ....

    Installed by: ....

Ceiling surface #3

    Type:..

    Rooms where found: ....

    Installation date: ....

    Installed by: ....

Ceiling surface #4

    Type:..

    Rooms where found: ....

    Installation date: ....

    Installed by: ....

Ceiling surface #5

    Type:..

    Rooms where found: ....

    Installation date: ....

    Installed by: ....

Wall Surfaces

Wall surface #1

    Type:..

    Rooms where found: ....

    Installation date: ....

    Installed by: ....

Wall surface #2

    Type:..

    Rooms where found: ....

    Installation date: ....

    Installed by: ....

Wall surface #3

    Type:..

    Rooms where found: ....

    Installation date: ....

    Installed by: ....

Wall surface #4

    Type:..

    Rooms where found: ....

    Installation date: ....

    Installed by: ....

Wall surface #5

    Type:..

    Rooms where found: ....

    Installation date: ....

    Installed by: ....

Ceiling/Wall Surface Inspection Log

Date Inspected	Problems Noted

Repairs & Maintenance

Date Inspected	Type of Repair

Professional Resources

Drywall installation/repair

#1:..
Tel: ....
Email:..

Plaster installation/repair

#1:..
Tel: ....
Email:..

Ceramic tile installation/repair

#1:..
Tel: ....
Email:..

Painter

#1:..
Tel: ....
Email:..
#2:..
Tel: ....
Email:..

Wall coverings

#1:..
Tel: ....
Email:..

Notes

_____
_____
_____
_____
_____

Walls, Ceiling & Trim (cont.) See page 23

Trim Molding Log

Trim Style #1

Type:...

Rooms where found:.......................................

Purchased from:..

Paint or stain:..

Trim Style #2

Type:...

Rooms where found:.......................................

Purchased from:..

Paint or stain:..

Trim Style #3

Type:...

Rooms where found:.......................................

Purchased from:..

Paint or stain:..

Trim Style #4

Type:...

Rooms where found:.......................................

Purchased from:..

Paint or stain:..

Professional Resources

#1:..

Tel:..

Email:...

#2:..

Tel:..

Email:...

Trimwork Inspection Log

Date Inspected	Problems Noted

Repairs & Maintenance

Date Inspected	Type of Repair

Window Treatments

Style #1

Rooms where located: ....

Manufacturer:..

Warranty: ....

Date of installation:...

Installed by: ....

Style #2

Rooms where located: ....

Manufacturer:..

Warranty: ....

Date of installation:...

Installed by: ....

Style #3

Rooms where located: ....

Manufacturer:..

Warranty: ....

Date of installation:...

Installed by: ....

Professional Resources

#1:...

Tel: ....

Email:..

#2:...

Tel: ....

Email:..

Notes

Flooring *See page 25*

Room	Type (carpet, wood, resilient, tile, other)	Age	Condition
Entry			
Mud/Utility			
Living			
Family			
Dining			
Kitchen			
Hall 1			
Hall 2			
Hall 3			
Bed 1			
Bed 2			
Bed 3			
Bed 4			
Bath 1			
Bath 2			
Bath 3			

Flooring Inspection Log

Date Inspected	Problems Noted

Professional Resources

#1: ....

    Tel: ....

    Email: ....

#2: ....

    Tel: ....

    Email: ....

Notes

Repairs & Maintenance

Date Inspected	Type of Repair

Electrical System *See pages 27–29*

Electrical Basics

Box type: ☐ Fuse ☐ Breaker

Service: ☐ 200 amp ☐ 150 amp ☐ 100 amp

Box location: ....

....

Power main shut-off location: ....

....

....

Electrical System Inspection Log

Date Inspected	Problems Noted

Repairs & Maintenance

Date Inspected	Type of Repair

For the chart below, note your meter reading for the current month. Record subsequent readings on the same day each month. Chart your usage to determine peaks, and plan conservation such as lowering electrical heating by two degrees, switching to CFL light bulbs throughout the house, or replacing aging appliances with Energy Star-rated models.

Meter location:..

Yearly Electrical Use											
Jan	**Feb**	**Mar**	**Apr**	**May**	**June**	**July**	**Aug**	**Sept**	**Oct**	**Nov**	**Dec**
90K											
80K											
30K											
20K											
10K											

Breaker Box Map

Circuit #	Type/Loads	Circuit #	Type/Loads
1		21	
2		22	
3		23	
4		24	
5		25	
6		26	
7		27	
8		28	
9		29	
10		30	
11		31	
12		32	
13		33	
14		34	
15		35	
16		36	
17		37	
18		38	
19		39	
20		40	

Receptacles & Fixtures *See page 31*

Receptacle Survey

Room	Standard	GFCI	TRR
Entry			
Mud/Utility			
Living			
Family			
Dining			
Kitchen			
Bath 1			
Bath 2			
Bath 3			
Bed 1			
Bed 2			
Bed 3			
Exterior			

Receptacle Inspection Log

Date Inspected	GFCI Tested?	Problems Noted

Repairs & Maintenance

Date Inspected	Type of Repair

Bulb Change Record

Room	Overhead	Wall	Lamp	Other
Entry				
Mud/Utility				
Living				
Family				
Dining				
Kitchen				
Bath 1				
Bath 2				
Bath 3				
Bed 1				
Bed 2				
Bed 3				
Exterior				

Notes

_____

_____

_____

_____

_____

_____

_____

_____

Water Supply System ✏ *See page 32*

Plumbing System Snapshot

Water source: ☐ Municipal ☐ Well

Wastewater system: ☐ Sewer ☐ Septic

Main water shut-off location:......................................

....

Plumbing professional used:......................................

....

   Tel: ....

   Email:..

Well Record

Pump type: ☐ Jet ☐ Jet, in well ☐ Submersible

Pump location: ....

Storage tank location: ....

....

Pressure switch location:.......................................

....

Control box/disconnect panel location (if any):............

....

Well serviced by:..

   Tel: ....

   Email:..

Well/Pump Inspection Log

Date Inspected	Problems Noted

Repairs & Maintenance

Date	Type of Repair

Notes

_____

_____

_____

_____

Water Usage Log

Date:	Date:	Date:	Date:	Date:	Date:	Date:
Meter Reading:	Meter Reading:	Meter Reading:	Meter Reading:	Meter Reading:	Meter Reading:	Meter Reading:
Date:	Date:	Date:	Date:	Date:	Date:	Date:
Meter Reading:	Meter Reading:	Meter Reading:	Meter Reading:	Meter Reading:	Meter Reading:	Meter Reading:
Date:	Date:	Date:	Date:	Date:	Date:	Date:
Meter Reading:	Meter Reading:	Meter Reading:	Meter Reading:	Meter Reading:	Meter Reading:	Meter Reading:
Date:	Date:	Date:	Date:	Date:	Date:	Date:
Meter Reading:	Meter Reading:	Meter Reading:	Meter Reading:	Meter Reading:	Meter Reading:	Meter Reading:
Date:	Date:	Date:	Date:	Date:	Date:	Date:
Meter Reading:	Meter Reading:	Meter Reading:	Meter Reading:	Meter Reading:	Meter Reading:	Meter Reading:
Date:	Date:	Date:	Date:	Date:	Date:	Date:
Meter Reading:	Meter Reading:	Meter Reading:	Meter Reading:	Meter Reading:	Meter Reading:	Meter Reading:
Date:	Date:	Date:	Date:	Date:	Date:	Date:
Meter Reading:	Meter Reading:	Meter Reading:	Meter Reading:	Meter Reading:	Meter Reading:	Meter Reading:
Date:	Date:	Date:	Date:	Date:	Date:	Date:
Meter Reading:	Meter Reading:	Meter Reading:	Meter Reading:	Meter Reading:	Meter Reading:	Meter Reading:
Date:	Date:	Date:	Date:	Date:	Date:	Date:
Meter Reading:	Meter Reading:	Meter Reading:	Meter Reading:	Meter Reading:	Meter Reading:	Meter Reading:

Water Treatment Systems ✎ *See pages 33–34*

Water Filter Record

Filtration type: ☐ Absorption ☐ UV
☐ Point-of-use ☐ Other

System location: ....

Inspection Log

Date Inspected	Problems Noted

Repairs & Maintenance

Date	Type of Repair

Water Softener Record

Softener location: ....

Installed: ....

Installer: ....

    Tel: ....

    Email: ....

Salt added:

    Date: ....

    Date: ....

    Date: ....

Water Heater Record

Water heater location: ....

Water heater type:

Capacity (conventional tank): ....gal.

Flow rate (tankless): ....gpm.

Brand/model: ....

Purchase date: ....

Purchased from: ....

Warranty: ....

Fuel source:

Installed by: ....

    Tel: ....

    Email: ....

Service done (including draining):

    Date: ....

    Date: ....

    Date: ....

    Date: ....

Sewer or Septic System

See page 37

Septic System Snapshot

System (tank) capacity: ....gal.

System map location: ....

System installed: ....

Dates pumped/cleaned:

    Date: ....

    Date: ....

    Date: ....

Septic contractor: ....

    Tel: ....

    Email: ....

Inspection Notes

....

....

....

....

....

....

....

....

....

....

....

Notes

Boiler or Furnace 🖉 *See page 39*

Home Heating Record

Type: ☐ Boiler ☐ Furnace

Fuel Source: ☐ Gas ☐ Electric

Unit original purchase:..

Make/model:..

Purchased from:..

AFUE rating: ....%

Serviced by:..

Tel:...

Warranty/gaurantee: ....

Utility service plan:...

Furnace Service Record
(including ductwork)

Date	Type of Repair

Filter Change Record

Filter Type:

    Manufacturer:...

    Model number:..

Recommended frequency: ....

Unit original purchase:.....................................

Dates filter changed:

    Date: ....

    Date: ....

    Date: ....

Furnace/boiler repair professional:.............................

....

    Tel: ....

    Email:..

Notes

_____
_____
_____
_____
_____
_____
_____
_____
_____
_____
_____

Air Conditioner 🖊 *See page 40*

Air Conditioning Record

Central air:

    Manufacturer:...

    Model number:...

Filter type:..

Filters cleaned/replaced:

    Date: ....

    Date: ....

    Date: ....

Coolant type:..

Recommended recharge frequency: ....

Recharge date record:

    Date: ....

    Date: ....

    Date: ....

Repair contractor: ....

    Tel: ....

    Email:..

Central Air Conditioner Service Record

Date	Type of Repair

Notes

_____

_____

_____

_____

_____

_____

_____

_____

_____

_____

_____

_____

_____

_____

_____

_____

_____

_____

_____

_____

_____

_____

_____

_____

_____

_____

_____

_____

HVAC System *See page 38*

Notes/Inspections for other Heating & Cooling system parts, including window air conditioners, space heaters, heated floors, air exchangers, heat pumps:

Safety & Security Systems See page 42

Fire Extinguishers

Extinguisher 1 location:..

Date acquired: ....

Date inspected: ....

Extinguisher 2 location:..

Date acquired: ....

Date inspected: ....

Extinguisher 3 location:..

Date acquired: ....

Date inspected: ....

Central Station Security System

Manufacturer:..

Service provider:..

Hint for access code:..

Hint for deactivation password: ....

Tel:..

Malfunctions/false alarms/maintenance: ....

....

....

....

....

....

Smoke Alarms

Smoke alarm 1 location: ....

Date installed: ....

Dates tested: ....

Battery change record:

Date:..

Date:..

Smoke alarm 2 location: ....

Date installed: ....

Dates tested: ....

Battery change record:

Date:..

Date:..

Smoke alarm 3 location: ....

Date installed: ....

Dates tested: ....

Battery change record:

Date:..

Date:..

Smoke alarm 4 location: ....

Date installed: ....

Dates tested: ....

Battery change record:

Date:..

Date:..

Notes

The Home Security Inspection Checklist

If you check, "No," for any of these, it is a cause for concern and an issue you need to address as soon as possible.

Entry doors either solid wood or metal? .... ☐ Yes ☐ No

Door hinges protected from removal from outside? .... ☐ Yes ☐ No

Door locks in good working order? .... ☐ Yes ☐ No

Deadbolt lock on side and back doors? .... ☐ Yes ☐ No

Door lock/handle blocked from window access .... ☐ Yes ☐ No

No window within 40 inches of lock/handle? .... ☐ Yes ☐ No

Windowless entry doors have peephole or viewer? .... ☐ Yes ☐ No

All home entrances lit with at least 40-watt bulb? .... ☐ Yes ☐ No

Window locks operable? .... ☐ Yes ☐ No

Window screens/storm windows lockable from inside? .... ☐ Yes ☐ No

Two door locks on back and side doors? .... ☐ Yes ☐ No

Front of house clear of obstructions such as bushes/shrubs? .... ☐ Yes ☐ No

Front entrance clearly observable from street? .... ☐ Yes ☐ No

Sliding glass doors lockable? .... ☐ Yes ☐ No

Clear line of sight from neighbors into backyard? .... ☐ Yes ☐ No

Any valuables locked up in garage? .... ☐ Yes ☐ No

Door from garage to house solid wood/metal and lockable? .... ☐ Yes ☐ No

Yard shed locked? .... ☐ Yes ☐ No

Upper floor windows inaccessible by garage or shed roof? .... ☐ Yes ☐ No

No ladders in yard, or accessible in shed/garage? .... ☐ Yes ☐ No

Exterior basement door secured with bar and lock? .... ☐ Yes ☐ No

Garage door lockable? .... ☐ Yes ☐ No

Garage windows lockable or fixed? .... ☐ Yes ☐ No

Appliances *See pages 43–46*

Refrigerator Record

Make/model: ....

Original purchase date: ....

Seller: ....

Extended warranty? ....

Manufacturer's warranty: ....

    Exp. date: ....

Capacity: .... cu. ft.

Maintenance notes: ....

....

....

Repairperson: ....

    Tel: ....

    Email: ....

Oven Record

Make/model: ....

Original purchase date: ....

Type: ....

Seller: ....

Extended warranty? ....

Manufacturer's warranty: ....

    Exp. date: ....

Maintenance notes: ....

....

....

Repairperson: ....

    Tel: ....

    Email: ....

Garbage Disposer Record

Make/model: ....

Original purchase date: ....

Seller: ....

Extended warranty? ....

Manufacturer's warranty: ....

    Exp. date: ....

Maintenance notes: ....

....

....

Repairperson: ....

    Tel: ....

    Email: ....

Notes

_____

_____

_____

_____

_____

_____

_____

_____

_____

_____

_____

_____

_____

Dishwasher Record

Make/model:..

Original purchase date:.................................

Seller:..

Extended warranty?.....................................

Manufacturer's warranty:...............................

    Exp. date:..

Maintenance notes:.....................................

....

....

Repairperson:..

    Tel: ....

    Email:...

Washing Machine Record

Make/model:..

Original purchase date:.................................

Seller:..

Extended warranty?.....................................

Manufacturer's warranty:...............................

    Exp. date:..

Maintenance notes:.....................................

....

....

Repairperson:..

    Tel: ....

    Email:...

Clothes Dryer Record

Make/model:..

Original purchase date:.................................

Seller:..

Extended warranty?.....................................

Manufacturer's warranty:...............................

    Exp. date:..

Maintenance notes:.....................................

....

....

Repairperson:..

    Tel: ....

    Email:...

Notes

Kitchen Notes

See pages 47–89 to record detailed data

Wall color: ....

Trim color: ....

Floor covering: ....

Ideas for furnishings and remodeling

Additional notes

Living Room Notes

See pages 47–89 to record detailed data

Wall color: ....

Trim color: ....

Floor covering: ....

Furniture: ....

Ideas for furnishings and remodeling

Additional notes

Bathroom #1 Notes *See pages 47–89 to record detailed data*

Wall color:..

Trim color:..

Floor covering:...

Ideas for furnishings and remodeling

Additional notes

Bathroom #2 Notes 🖊 See pages 47–89 to record detailed data

Wall color:..

Trim color:..

Floor covering:..

Ideas for furnishings and remodeling

Additional notes

Bedroom #1 Notes

See pages 47–89 to record detailed data

Wall color:..

Trim color:..

Floor covering:..

Furniture:..

Ideas for furnishings and remodeling

Additional notes

Bedroom #2 Notes

See pages 47–89 to record detailed data

Wall color: ....

Trim color: ....

Floor covering: ....

Furniture: ....

Ideas for furnishings and remodeling

Additional notes

Bedroom #3 Notes

See pages 47–89 to record detailed data

Wall color:...

Trim color:...

Floor covering:...

Furniture:...

Ideas for furnishings and remodeling

Additional notes

Bedroom/Spare Room Notes

See pages 47–89 to record detailed data

Wall color: ....

Trim color: ....

Floor covering: ....

Furniture: ....

Ideas for furnishings and remodeling

Additional notes/rooms

Family Room Notes

See pages 47–89 to record detailed data

Wall color:..

Trim color:..

Floor covering:..

Furniture:...

Ideas for furnishings and remodeling

Additional notes

Workshop/Garage Notes

See pages 47–89 to record detailed data

Ideas for improving and upgrading

Additional notes/outbuildings

Additional Notes

Home Inventory

Fire, theft, natural disasters, and other emergencies are all thankfully rare. But that doesn't mean they don't happen. When damage or loss occurs, you'll turn to your homeowner's insurance (and, in some cases, state and federal assistance) to make your home whole again. That's when a home inventory is most crucial.

But it's also good to know what you have and where. An inventory inevitably gives you some idea of what you want to upgrade.

The form that follows is highly detailed; you may not be able to provide all the information. That's okay. As long as any item can be identified from your description, chances are that a replacement value can be determined. The form is exhaustive, so simply ignore listings that don't apply. You don't have to list things that have little or no relative value (i.e., that thrift shop end table leftover from your first apartment).

Appliances	Make	Model	Style	Age	Purch $/value
Refrigerator					
Range/oven					
Microwave					
Dishwasher					
Garbage disposal					
Trash compactor					
Toaster oven					
Coffee/espresso maker					
Washing machine					
Dryer					
Dehumidifier					
Air purifier					
Water filtration system					
Small appliance 1					

Electronics	Make	Model	Style	Age	Purch $/value
Computer 1					
Computer 2					
Peripheral 1					
Peripheral 2					
Printer					
Fax					

Electronics	Make	Model	Style	Age	Purch $/value
Scanner					
TV 1					
TV 2					
TV 3					
Game console					
DVD player					
Cable modem					
Wireless router					
Stereo					
Speakers					
Home entertainment system					
Camera					
Video camera					

System Fixtures	Make	Model	Style	Age	Purch $/value
Central A/C unit					
Sump pump					
Water heater					
Boiler/furnace					
Wall/window A/C 1					
Wall/window A/C 2					
Wall/window A/C 3					

Personal	Source	Material	Style	Age	Purch $/value
Jewelry 1 (group as necessary)					
Jewelry 2 (group as necessary)					

Home Inventory (cont.)

Personal	Source	Material	Style	Age	Purch $/value
Jewelry 3 (group as necessary)					
Jewelry 4 (group as necessary)					
Art 1 (group as necessary)					
Art 2 (group as necessary)					
Art 3 (group as necessary)					
Collectible 1 (group as necessary)					
Collectible 2 (group as necessary)					
Collectible 3 (group as necessary)					
Crystal					

Personal	Source	Material	Style	Age	Purch $/value
China					
Formal flatware					
Valuable Clothing 1 (group as necessary)					
Valuable Clothing 2 (group as necessary)					
Valuable Clothing 3 (group as necessary)					
Valuable Clothing 4 (group as necessary)					
Valuable Clothing 5 (group as necessary)					
Wine (group as appropriate)					

Personal	Source	Material	Style	Age	Purch $/value
Musical instrument 1 (group as necessary)					
Musical instrument 2 (group as necessary)					
Musical instrument 3 (group as necessary)					

Furnishings	Make	Model/material	Size/Style	Age	Purch $/value
Sofa/couch/ loveseat 1					
Sofa/couch/ loveseat 2					
Sofa/couch/ loveseat 3					
Bed 1					
Bed 2					
Bed 3					

Furnishings	Make	Model/material	Size/Style	Age	Purch $/value
Kitchen table					
Dining room table					
Chandelier					
Coffee table					
Accent Table 1					
Accent Table 2					
Accent Table 3					
Desk 1					
Desk 2					
Chair 1					

Home Inventory (cont.)

Furnishings	Make	Model/material	Size/Style	Age	Purch $/value
Chair 2					
Chair 3					
Chair 4					
Wardrobe					
Lamp 1 (group as necessary)					
Lamp 2 (group as necessary)					
Lamp 3 (group as necessary)					
Exercise equip. 1 (group as necessary)					
Exercise equip. 2 (group as necessary)					

Yard, Garden & Garage	Make	Model/material	Style	Age	Purch $/value
Lawn mower					
String trimmer					
Power tool 1 (group as necessary)					
Power tool 2 (group as necessary)					
Power tool 3 (group as necessary)					
Woodworking tool 1 (group as necessary)					
Woodworking tool 2 (group as necessary)					
Woodworking tool 3 (group as necessary)					
Hand tool 1 (group as necessary)					

Yard, Garden & Garage	Make	Model/material	Style	Age	Purch $/value
Hand tool 2 (group as necessary)					
Hand tool 3 (group as necessary)					
Hand tool 4 (group as necessary)					
Hand tool 5 (group as necessary)					

Miscellaneous	Make	Model	Style	Age	Purch $/value
Misc. 1					
Misc. 2					
Misc. 3					
Misc. 4					
Misc. 5					
Misc. 6					
Misc. 7					
Misc. 8					
Misc. 9					
Misc.10					
Misc.11					
Misc.12					
Misc. 13					
Misc. 14					
Misc. 15					
Misc. 16					
Misc. 17					
Misc. 18					

Other Important Household Data

Other Important Household Data (cont.)

Other Important Household Data (cont.)

Other Important Household Data (cont.)

Other Important Household Data (cont.)

Resources

Air Conditioning, Heating, and Refrigeration Institute
Consumer information for the homeowner, regarding residential HVAC systems, and an explanation of SEER rating.

www.ari.org
(703) 524-8800

Angie's List
Paid membership site featuring homeowner reviews of goods and service providers operating locally.

www.angieslist.com

The Associated General Contractors of America
Includes a searchable member directory on their website.

www.agc.org

Chimney Safety Institute of America
Safety and care information for homeowners, news and education information about chimney-related issues, and listing of certified professional chimney sweeps by location.

www.csia.org
(317) 837-5362

Electrical Safety Foundation International
Provides in-depth information on home electrical safety, inspections, and home electrical systems.

efsi.org
(703) 841-3229

Federal Emergency Management Agency (FEMA)
Information about emergency procedures for different catastrophic events, as well as instructions to make your home safer and to prepare for emergencies.

www.fema.gov
800-621- FEMA (3362)

National Association of Home Builders (NAHB)
Comprehensive guidance for the home on buying, building, financing, maintaining, and remodeling a home. Includes a list of members nationwide.

www.nahb.org
(800) 368-5242

National Association of the Remodeling Industry
Information about budgeting for, planning for, and getting the most out of a home remodeling project. Searchable listing of contractors.

www.nari.org
847-298-9200

National Association of Wastewater Transporters
The website provides a list of reputable local septic tank inspectors and pumpers.

www.nawt.org

National Ground Water Association
Provides news and information about ground water contamination and solutions to keeping ground water in wells clean.

www.ngwa.org
(800) 551-7379

National Safety Foundation
Dedicated to educating consumers on safety in the products they buy and use, as well as safe practices—and other issues such as food safety.

www.nsf.com
(734) 769-8010

National Tile Contractors Association
Listing of tile contractors, tile suppliers, and other resources for the homeowner.

www.tile-assn.com
(601) 939-2071

Painting and Decorating Contractors of America
Industry group for home painting and decorating contractors, and includes a "find a painter" search feature.

www.pdca.org
(800) 332-7322